D0058640

Russ & Daughters

Russ & Daughters

Reflections and Recipes from the House That Herring Built

WITHDRAWN

Mark Russ Federman

Foreword by Calvin Trillin

SCHOCKEN BOOKS, NEW YORK

Copyright © 2013 by Mark Federman
Foreword copyright © 2013 by Calvin Trillin

All rights reserved. Published in the United States by Schocken Books, a division of Random House, Inc., New York, and in Canada by Random House of Canada Limited, Toronto.

Schocken Books and colophon are registered trademarks of Random House, Inc.

Unless otherwise indicated, all photographs are courtesy of the author and Russ & Daughters. Color photographs copyright © Belathée Photography.

Grateful acknowledgment is made to Columbia University Press for permission to reprint "The Soul of a Store" by Mark Russ Federman from *Gastropolis: Food and New York City,* edited by Annie Hauck-Lawson and Jonathan Deutsch. Copyright © 2009 by Columbia University Press. Reprinted with permission of the publisher.

Library of Congress Cataloging-in-Publication Data
Federman, Mark Russ.
Russ & Daughters : reflections and recipes from the house that herring built / Mark Russ Federman ; foreword by Calvin Trillin.
p. cm.
ISBN 978-0-8052-4294-2 (hardback)
1. Russ & Daughters—History. 2. Appetizers—New York (State)—New York. 3. Jewish cooking—New York (State)—New York. I. Title.
TX945.5.R86 2013 641.5'676—dc23 2012023902

www.schocken.com

Jacket photographs by Lesley Unruh
Jacket design by Kelly Blair

Printed in the United States of America
First Edition
2 4 6 8 9 7 5 3 1

To Hattie, Ida, and Anne—the Russ Daughters

Without them, there would be no store and no stories

CONTENTS

FOREWORD BY CALVIN TRILLIN

When my daughters were small, I used to go to Russ & Daughters on Sunday mornings to have them appreciated. Oh, sure, I'd buy some smoked salmon while I was there. I'd get a little whitefish salad. I might buy a smoked trout or two. On some Sundays, I would spend a few minutes pondering my father's dismissal of chopped herring as the sort of thing Litvaks (Jews from Lithuania) eat; my father, who was brought as an infant to Missouri from the Ukraine, considered Litvaks, including my maternal grandmother and her entire family, faintly risible. Then I'd get some chopped herring. I might treat myself to some pickled lox. (Yes, of course, with cream and onions; it is customary for me to eat everything with everything.) It was all merchandise of the highest quality, of course—all the more delectable to me because of having endured a childhood without such food in Kansas City, where, as one of my daughters observed at the age of four, the bagels just taste like round bread. Still, I was there to have my daughters appreciated, and in that endeavor I was never disappointed.

At Russ & Daughters a particularly adorable two-year-old didn't get the quick smile and cursory "Isn't she dear" that you might hear from, say, the proprietor of an English tearoom. The daughters of Joel Russ, The Founder, were running the place then, along with their husbands, and they were people who had fully absorbed the profound teaching of Willy Loman's wife: "Attention must be paid." Am I just imagining it, or did one of them, while emerging from behind the counter to get within cheek-pinching range of one of my daughters, sometimes say to her colleagues, "How can you stand there and slice fish with a face like that in the store?" Once, when my girls were still small, a friend of mine informed me that he had found a smoked-salmon supplier in the Canadian Maritimes who shipped superb salmon at much lower than

New York prices. "No, thank you," I said. "There are some things that cannot be done by mail."

While the salmon was being sliced, I would entertain my daughters with my only magic trick, palming gummy-fish and pretending to pull one out of one of their ears. Then we would go next door to Ben's Dairy, a tiny store that was run by a strong-minded man who once responded to a French embargo on spare parts for Israeli jets by putting up a sign that said UNTIL GENERAL DE GAULLE CHANGES HIS POLICY TOWARD ISRAEL, BEN SELLS NO MORE FRENCH CHEESE. At Ben's we'd get cream cheese and a loaf of baked farmer's cheese with scallions. Then we'd go next door to Tanenbaum's Bakery, where we purchased, among other baked goods, some gnarly and oniony little black pumpernickel bagels that my older daughter devoured on Sunday and dreamed of for the rest of the week.

Ben's Dairy and Tanenbaum's are long gone, most of their specialties folded into the Russ & Daughters inventory. My daughters grew up, left for college, and eventually started families of their own. But Russ & Daughters still looks about the same as it did when I described it, around forty years ago, as a refutation of the false teaching that a store that sells pickled herring cannot have character and a clean display case at the same time. There have been some changes, of course. The store shopping bag, for instance, has a contemporary design and no longer bears the old motto "Queens of Lake Sturgeon." The shelves include some upscale items that would not have been familiar to The Founder. Still, in the hands of the fourth generation of Russes, Russ & Daughters is essentially unchanged. I know, because I can often be found there on a Sunday morning.

My salmon is still sliced by Herman Vargas, the rare Yiddish-speaking Dominican, who has worked at Russ & Daughters for more than thirty years; I know him as Herman the Artistic Slicer, although he no longer wears a name badge identifying him as that. On Sundays these days, while waiting for Herman to produce slices thin enough to read *The New York Times* through—not the big-print edition; I'm talking about the regular—I pretend to pull gummy-fish out of the ears of my grandchildren. They have been brought to Russ & Daughters to be appreciated.

INTRODUCTION

It's hard to forget your ancestors when they're staring down at you from the walls above the top shelves. Some of the portraits are near the olives, others are by the dried-fruit baskets, and some are next to the caviar display. Not only are they staring down, but they're also passing judgment: "The showcase glass has fingerprint smudges." "The lox knives and cutting board need to be wiped clean." "The pickled herrings have to be filled in." "Why isn't somebody answering the phone?" Some—if not most—days, you'd like to forget them, especially when you're tired. But we're the Russ family. We're not allowed to be tired. We have been selling herring, lox, caviar, and candy on the Lower East Side of New York City for one hundred years. From the frames above the shelves, the ancestral message is clear: "We're only as good as our last quarter pound of lox." This is our *yichis.*

Yichis is Yiddish for "pedigree," or "lineage," and in Jewish tradition it means having notable rabbinic ancestors, or ancestors who were community leaders of whatever European village or town your family came from. That mantle is usually passed down from generation to generation along the male line. But Yiddish is a language that adapts itself to the usually temporary residences of Jews who have been forced for the last thousand years from one place to another. And so, on the Lower East Side, *yichis* has been used to describe any family business that has had the rare good fortune to survive the generational transfer from father to son. In our case, the business was originally passed down not from father to son but from father to daughters. In our family there is no royalty—no rabbis, no community leaders. We are clearly peasant stock, and what is being passed down is not religion but fish: smoked, cured, and pickled.

This is our *yichis,* the hard work and the satisfaction of selling herring: of getting the fish into the store each morning, of arranging the displays hundreds of times each day, of customers buying and countermen selling, and, it is to be hoped, of making a profit in the process.

I am now sixty-seven years old and have passed the business on to the next generation. I was the transitional generation. I took over the family fish store at a time when both the business and the neighborhood were in decline. I inherited a mom-and-pop business model and a Depression-era mentality. And I struggled, much like the generations before me, to keep the business alive. Now, no longer the "Mr. Russ" in charge, I have the opportunity to reflect rather than react. I can think about all of the changes that my family has witnessed over the past one hundred years from behind the counter of our appetizing store on the Lower East Side. In my retirement, I no longer have to stand behind the counter; I get to sit on the bench in front of the store under the neon sign Grandpa Russ installed in 1950.

The top line of the sign reads RUSS & DAUGHTERS in green neon. The bottom line, in red neon, reads APPETIZERS. They are flanked by tricolor—white, yellow, and blue—neon fish. The fish are of indeterminate species. Some people might think they look like herring; others may be sure they are whitefish or salmon. That's fine with us; we're not sure what they are, either.

What the sign does not say is "Since 1914." For my grandfather, who founded the store, and his three daughters and their husbands, who ran the store until I took over thirty-five years ago, this wasn't important at the time. Longevity was measured in months and years, certainly not in decades. Staying in business was a struggle, a matter of survival. Now, in 2012, it seems impressive. Ninety-nine years in business is something to be proud of. It's actually 106 years, if you start counting in 1907, the year Grandpa Russ arrived in this country and filled his first pushcart with herring on Hester Street on the Lower East Side. But why quibble? Let's split the difference and call it a hundred.

The Lower East Side of 2012 bears no resemblance to the Jewish ghetto where my grandfather arrived in 1907. Almost everything has changed. Our customers are no longer just Eastern European Jews. They come from every ethnic group in America, and from all over the world. We now get both the subway set and the jet set. Our products

The Russ & Daughters storefront

have become mainstream. The once humble herring is now haute cuisine. And who doesn't like bagels and lox? While we once did business strictly across the counter, we now sell our products across cyberspace. Our neighborhood has gone from squalid ghetto to tenement chic. And the hardworking Russ family has changed, too. We are now hardworking and have advanced university degrees.

Yet for all of the changes, there are some things that haven't changed at all. We still work with our hands. We may take orders over the Internet, but the fish is still sliced and filleted by hand, wrapped by hand, and packed for shipping by hand. We still give personal attention to our customers. We know many of them by name, and we know the names of their spouses, children, and pets. We remember their joys and their sorrows, and we listen as they tell us about both, dispensing advice when needed. It has been said that New York has a love affair with Russ & Daughters. It is equally true that Russ & Daughters is in love with New York and New Yorkers.

But you don't have to be a New Yorker—nor do you need to be Jewish—to understand and appreciate our family's story. Every immigrant group has a similar story: first the struggle to survive and then to make its way into the American mainstream. And each community cherishes its own specialty food stores that have helped it retain and celebrate a part of its unique culture. It's the store you went to with your mother or father, grandmother or grandfather, where you were greeted by the owner with a pat on the head or a pinch of the cheek, where you breathed in an aroma that has become part of your sensory memory, an aroma that you carried into your house with the shopping bags full of goodies that would be shared with your family and extended family on special occasions. Today you search for the smells, the tastes, and the experiences of shopping in these beloved stores. You yearn to recapture the feeling of those shopping trips, when customer, counterman, and product came together in a unique moment. Something other than money and fish changing hands across a counter was going on here. This is what the Russ family has worked so hard to maintain. This is the soul of our store. And this is why I wrote this book.

Russ & Daughters

I

Our History, Sliced Thin

Six days a week, ten hours a day, for thirty years, I walked back and forth between the tiny office at the rear of the store and the glass showcases filled with perfectly trimmed smoked fish, herrings submerged in brines and sauces, a dozen fresh salads, and cream cheese trays. Next to the showcases were overflowing bagel and bialy bins alongside stacks of rye and pumpernickel breads. And off to the side were sparkling glass jars full of dried fruit, nuts, and candies. Spotless scales, knives, and counters completed the picture.

This was the very same walk that my grandparents, parents, aunts, and uncles took many times a day when they owned and operated Russ & Daughters. Now the fourth generation—my daughter, Niki, and my nephew Josh—make these same rounds as I transition into retirement.

It's a short walk from the back of the store to the front. Most of the time.

"You! Get behind da counter and make me a schmaltz herring!"

An elderly woman pushed her way out of the crowd of waiting customers and cut me off like a motorcycle cop.

"I'm sorry, what number are you?"

"Vhat number? I haf never taken a number. I haf been shopping here for seventy years. I can't vait. Get behind da counter and make me a herring."

This lady was obviously unaware of the fact that the business was now in the hands of the fourth generation of the Russ family, that I no longer went behind the counter to sell herring, that I had proclaimed myself "Herring Maven Emeritus." But it wouldn't have made any difference to her anyway. She clearly had never taken a number or waited in line for anything in her life. So I went behind the counter and reached for a herring in the middle of the tray—knowing that this woman would never, *ever* buy a herring off the top; not from the top of the showcase tray and, when the herrings were sold out of large wooden barrels in front of our store, not from the top of the barrel. For this type of customer I had to go fishing. I selected a herring from the middle of the tray, a particularly large and fat—schmaltzy—herring with clear, shiny blue-gray skin, a broad back, and a belly full of roe. As I removed it from the showcase, she started in again.

"Vhat? Vhat are you doing?! Vhat do I look like? You tink I don't know herring? I've been eating herring since before you vere born. I ate herring on da udder side—dat was real herring! Now make me a herring. It should be a nice one. I don't haf all day."

What was I thinking? The type of customer who wouldn't buy a herring off the top would *never* buy the first herring chosen by the counterman. Even if the counterman happened to be the owner and the third generation of the Russ family, who has been selling herrings on the Lower East Side since 1907. I would have to work for this sale. Why didn't I just tell her to take what I gave her and stop making a nuisance of herself? Because I grew up in a culture where the customer is king—or, in this case, queen. Because, in all honesty, I'm drawn to this type of customer—the old-timer who is fast becoming an endangered species. I love these characters. Rolling up my sleeves, I reached farther down into the middle of the tray of schmaltz herrings. I pulled out another herring that was largely indistinguishable from the one that had been rejected. I held it up and displayed it for her as if she was buying a diamond.

"Now, *dat's* a herring." She smiled, and I was somewhat pleased with myself, having satisfied this tough customer after only two attempts. It often took much longer with an old-timer. I hadn't lost my touch.

I placed the chosen herring on a long sheet of wet wax paper to be wrapped. Years ago, before the existence of the Food and Drug Administration, the Department of Agriculture, and the Department of Consumer Affairs, the herring would have been wrapped in old newspapers: usually the *Forverts* (Forward) or *Der Tog* (The Day) by my grandfather, or the *New York Herald-Tribune* or *The Daily Mirror* by my parents. Even in the beginning of my career as a fishmonger, I wrapped herring in *The New York Times.* As far as I know, no one ever died or even became sick from eating herring wrapped in newspaper. But now federal, state, and city laws require wax paper and plastic wrapping. So that's what we do.

"Vhat! Vhat are you doing?" Her voice became even more agitated. The other customers were now watching.

"I'm wrapping your herring."

"I said you should *make* me a herring. Take off da skin, take out da bones, and make sure you take out *all* da bones. Mine grandchildren are coming."

"We have schmaltz herrings already filleted," I said, pointing to a tray of fillets and reaching in, hoping to win her acceptance with the first or second one I chose. By now everyone, including the employees, was focused on the little old lady, the schmaltz herrings, and me. The store grew more crowded as my employees stared at us, the phones went unanswered, and the customers waited.

"Look at this tray of beautiful herrings. They were just filleted, not more than an hour ago. I have fifty people working in the kitchen; forty of them do nothing all day but fillet schmaltz herring. This is not done by machine but by hand. They are experts. Every piece of skin is trimmed off; every bone removed. I have their hands insured by Lloyd's of London." The situation called for some hyperbole.

"I vant you should *MAKE* me a herring. Now!"

Coming from this customer, "make" was a command of biblical import.

I was losing my patience. She was taking up too much of my time. Filleting a herring is time-consuming work. Customers as well as employees waited for the climax of this Jewish standoff.

I went for the ultimate weapon in my arsenal. "Lady, do you know who I am?"

She looked at me quizzically, one eyebrow raised, waiting to hear who I thought I was.

"I am Mr. Russ." I expected my pronouncement to end any further challenges.

It took less than a second for her response. "I know you. You're not Mistar Russ. Your grandfadder vas Mistar Russ."

She was right, of course. My grandfather, the real Mr. Russ, would have filleted the herring for her. No questions asked. It was, in fact, herring that brought him to America. Herring supported his family. Herring was how the Russ family survived in America. I was defeated. There was no choice but to fillet the whole schmaltz herring. I MADE her a herring. And, truth be told, I was actually happy to do it.

Gathering the Story

From the early 1880s to the mid-1920s, about three million Jews came to America from Eastern Europe. They fled poverty and pogroms, leaving their shtetlach in search of a better life. Among those people was my grandfather Joel Russ, who came from Strzyzov (Strzyżów in Polish), which was in an area known as Galicia, then part of the Austro-Hungarian Empire and now in southeastern Poland. While that sounds fairly regal, Strzyzov was a poor village and the Russes were among its poorest families. In its heyday Strzyzov had two thousand residents, half of whom were Jewish. After World War II and the Holocaust, no Jews were left in Strzyzov.

What was life like in the Old Country? Grandpa Russ refused to talk about his life before he came to America. Fortunately, two of the three Russ daughters, my mother, Anne, now ninety, and Aunt Hattie, now ninety-nine, are alive, living in Florida, and as lucid as ever. (The third Russ sister, my aunt Ida, also lived there until she died in 2001 at the age of eighty-six.) They, of course, attribute their mental acuity to eating lots of fish: smoked, cured, and pickled.

Getting them to reminisce requires me to visit Florida. Their gated community has a golf course, swimming pools, and tennis courts, but it still reminds me of Grandpa Russ's shtetl: those who live within its confines are like-minded people dealing with an ever-present fear, in this case not of poverty or pogroms but of old age and death. Florida is filled with many such shtetlach.

Visiting my mother and aunts was challenging when they first moved south. I was expected to stop at each of the three apartments on the first day of my arrival for a meal—or, at the very least, some rugelach, a cup of tea, and a piece of fruit. God forbid I should turn down anything they offered me. While I ate, they fussed about in perpetual motion, asking me questions, keeping my plate full, cleaning the dishes, and straightening the room—a direct result, I suppose, of years behind the counter waiting on customers, filling in the showcases, and cleaning the scales and knives. I am now their only connection to the business that was such a big part of their lives. They wanted to know if Mrs. Goldberg was still alive, if Mrs. Schwartz was still married to that *farbissener* (sourpuss) husband of hers, whether the Rubenstein twins ever got married. ("Such a shame, they never had their teeth fixed.")

Their Florida apartments contain little evidence of the lives they lived as they migrated from the Lower East Side to Brooklyn, then back to the Lower East Side, then to the suburbs, and finally to high-rise condos in Manhattan. There are a few pieces of furniture and a vase or two that have been schlepped along to each location because of some emotional connection that was never explained to me. There are the requisite tchotchke cabinets that now display only a few Hummel figurines or a porcelain dog collection. All of the souvenirs from trips to Niagara Falls or Israel are long gone. On the walls are framed photos of their children, grandchildren, great-grandchildren, and late husbands. The walls also have an ever-growing number of framed needlepoints, products of hands that refuse to remain idle in retirement. There is the swan-shaped candy dish that made the north-to-south trip and is always filled with the same recognizable candies: coffee Nips, Crystal Mints, and sour lemons. Their dentists tell them not to eat hard candies. Their doctors tell them to "lay off the salt." They pay no attention. There is a coffee table with a stack of large-print books. Their apartments look down over golf courses and tennis courts. (Though they don't play golf or tennis, it has always been about "location.") They had big homes up north and now have no need for large living spaces. They have made it clear to their children: there will be no assisted-living facilities, no nursing homes. They will each finish their lives in their own apartments in Florida. "All the arrangements have been made," they tell us. "Everything is paid for."

To make it easy for myself, I used to take them out to their favorite fish restaurant for the early-bird special. This had its own problems, as the entire community of golden agers usually ate at the same restaurants at the same times and had the same hearing problems. With everyone shouting at everyone else, it was difficult to have a conversation.

Visiting has become easier now that my mother and Aunt Hattie are no longer very mobile. But getting them to remember their youth is often a challenge. I have come to understand that their lives on the Lower East Side were difficult and that they would prefer not to relive them. They see my persistent questioning as an annoyance. "Life was very hard; what's to remember?" they have said to me in unison. (Getting the Russ sisters to agree on anything—even after decades of working and living together—should be considered a minor miracle.) If I go to Aunt Hattie with a question, her initial response is "Why are you bothering me with that? Go ask your mother; she's younger, she has a better memory." And when I go to my mother with the same question, she says, "Why are you bothering me with that? Ask your aunt Hattie; she's older, she'll remember." I have also learned that if we share a meal—some nova, a bit of sturgeon, and soft bialys—that I bring with me from Russ & Daughters, the memories do come. But when they talk about the "old days," I note that they don't call them "the good old days."

On my most recent visit, I asked my mother and Aunt Hattie to tell me what they knew about their father's life in the Old Country. "Not much. Papa was sent out of the house at age nine to be an apprentice to a shoemaker. Later he walked to Germany to apprentice as a baker. He came from Strzyzov in Galicia. He never spoke of it. Life was very hard. He didn't want to remember it. We didn't want to ask." There would not be much information here. I was on my own.

The Strzyzover Rebbe

At about the same time I was thinking about Strzyzov and my lost family history, I was also thinking about buying a new exercise bike. It seemed impractical to buy a huge piece of expensive equipment over the Internet; the shipping would be costly, and putting it together a headache. So my wife, Maria, and I began making the rounds of local fitness-equipment stores, including one in the Borough Park section of Brooklyn that was owned and staffed by Hasidic Jews. Our salesman there was the archetypal *yeshiva bocher,* a student of the holy books. Tall, skinny, pale, and with a wispy beard, he was clearly not an athlete. There was no chance that this fellow had spent any time on the equipment he was selling, which was in sharp contrast to the salesman at the previous fitness store we had visited on Long Island. The action figure–like salesman there clearly had an intimate relationship with his machines, and probably with steroids as well. Neither fellow was a particularly good advertisement for the equipment he was selling.

We left the Brooklyn fitness store without an exercise bike and decided to take a walk on New Utrecht Avenue, a nearby bustling shopping area under the elevated train tracks. Borough Park, once a culturally mixed community of Jews, Italians, and Irish, has become a fairly insular community of Hasidic Jews, who have one of the highest birthrates in the city. To those from outside this world, even to non-Hasidic Jews, this part of Brooklyn looks like a homogeneous community of Hasidim who all dress alike, look alike, and no doubt think alike. In fact, there are multiple sects within the community: Bobov, Belz, Ger, Satmar, Stolin, Vizhnitz, Munkacz, Spinka, Klausenburg, Skver, and Puppa Hasidim all reside here. There are subtle differences in their style of dress and their manner of prayer, but the most significant distinction involves the rabbinic leaders of each sect, to whom their followers are completely devoted.

As we were walking, I noticed a store that sold prepared food and had a glatt kosher (the most stringent level of *kashrut*) sign in the window. Everything looked freshly made and was nicely displayed. When we went inside, we were impressed by the variety of foods, many of which were familiar to me from my childhood: kasha varnishkes; stuffed derma; chopped liver; fried, boiled, stewed, and baked chicken; four versions of eggplant salad; several cabbage creations; and countless potato-based products. The staff was made up of older Jews and an equal number of young Mexicans. The Jewish employees wore yarmulkes; the Mexicans wore baseball caps.

We were waited on by one of the Mexicans, but all of our questions were being answered by one of the Jews who stood beside him: "You should buy the baked chicken. I just brought some home last night and my wife said it was better than hers. Why not buy a little eggplant salad? It goes perfect with the chicken." He was clearly one of the owners. I engaged him in conversation.

"I'm impressed by your shop. The food looks very appetizing."

"Thanks."

"And I should know, I'm in the appetizing business."

"You sell lox and herring?"

"Yes."

His eyes lit up. "I love herring. Do you have a store?"

"Yes."

"Where?"

"On the Lower East Side." At this point in the conversation I expected him to come right out with "Russ & Daughters?" Most people do.

"What's the name of your store?" He didn't get it yet.

"Russ & Daughters." No response. Not even a glimmer of recognition. He had never heard of it. I was deflated. Almost everyone in New York City, Jewish or not, knows the name Russ & Daughters. But on reflection, it wasn't so strange at all. I was in the heart of Hasidic Brooklyn. Our store has always been located on the Lower East Side of Manhattan. But it wasn't just the geographical separation. From its very beginnings, Russ & Daughters was not strictly kosher but, rather, simply "kosher style." The worlds of "glatt kosher" and "kosher style" are two gastronomic realms that never, ever meet.

"Mark Russ Federman." I held out my hand for a formal greeting.

"Yankie Rubin." He shook my hand with genuine enthusiasm.

"Your store sign says 'Meisner's.' Who's Meisner?"

"He's my partner." Now it was established, store owner talking to store owner.

"Your food is familiar to me," I said. "We're Galitzianers. My people are from Strzyzov."

Yankie became excited. "Strzyzov? The Strzyzover shul is one block from here. The Strzyzover Rebbe lives there, too. He's a customer."

I was floored by this stroke of luck. "You're kidding!" I said. "I've been trying to get some information about Strzyzov." My heart almost stopped. This was *bashert,* which is Yiddish for "fate," "destiny," or "meant to be."

"Call me tomorrow and I'll see if I have a phone number for him. He's a very old man."

Even better, I thought.

The following day, a Friday, I called Yankie Rubin, who gave me the Strzyzover Rebbe's phone number. I called immediately, so I could reach the rabbi before the Sabbath began. A woman answered the phone and launched into an interrogation when I asked to speak with the rabbi.

"Who are you?"

"My name is Mark Federman. I got the rabbi's number from Yankie Rubin, the owner of Meisner's food store on New Utrecht."

"Who?"

"Yankie Rubin."

"What?"

"Meisner's."

"Where?"

"Under the El," I said, raising my voice, thinking she either didn't hear or didn't understand me.

"Oh. And why do you want to speak to the rabbi?" She was clearly the gatekeeper.

"I'm writing a book about my family, the Russ family; we have been in business on the Lower East Side for one hundred years. I would like to find out whatever I can about Strzyzov, where my grandfather came from. Perhaps the rabbi can be of some help."

"When did your grandfather come here?"

"1907."

"And you want the rabbi should know what happened a hundred years ago?"

The lady was dead serious.

"No, I don't expect him to have any direct knowledge, but maybe he knows stories or has books or pictures." I decided to try a different approach. "And who am I talking to?" I asked.

"I am the rabbi's wife," she said in a different tone of voice, one with a certain practiced, lofty air.

"Oh, the rebbetzin," I replied. It was an opportunity to use one of the few Yiddish words I had in my limited vocabulary.

She was unimpressed. "You can call the rabbi tomorrow." For her, the conversation was over.

"But tomorrow is Shabbos." I thought she might be old and forgetful.

"No!" she said, clearly leaving out but obviously thinking, *You moron!* "Tomorrow night at nine fifteen." She was probably wondering why she had to explain this self-evident fact to a Jew.

The following night, at 9:15, I did call the rabbi. Once again, the rebbetzin answered, but she quickly put the rabbi on the phone.

"Rabbi"—I decided not to use the familiar form, "Rebbe," quite yet—"I suppose your wife told you why I'm calling."

"Yes?" This was somewhere between a declaration and a question, but I wasn't sure which.

"My grandfather came from Strzyzov and established a business on the Lower East Side in 1907. We are still on the Lower East Side and still in business more than a hundred years later. Four generations selling herring and smoked fish." I thought I might soften him up with the possibility of a payoff in food, but he cut me off.

"I don't eat so much anymore. I have a bad stomach, diabetes." He went on with a litany of ailments, as if he thought I was a doctor doing a medical workup. So much for the food bribe, which I realized wouldn't have worked anyway: he was glatt kosher; we are kosher style.

"Well, I thought that since you are the Strzyzover Rebbe, you might be able to help me with—" He cut me off again.

"Are you an old man?" This question caught me off guard, but I thought it might be his attempt to be friendly.

"It depends. I'm sixty-four, but I think of myself as young. I'm in pretty good shape, thank God." (I threw in the "thank God," a phrase I don't often use, to get on his good side.) "How about you, Rebbe?" Now I slipped into the familiar, thinking we had formed a relationship.

"You plus tventy. Vhere do you live?" Maybe he was warming to me.

"I live in Brooklyn. In Park Slope."

He seemed to give this some thought. "Oh. Dat's vhere dey have de expensive houses?"

"Well, I bought my house about thirty years ago. I couldn't afford to buy it now. Who could afford a house in Park Slope selling herrings? Now, about Strzyzov—"

"I vas not born in Strzyzov. I only vent dere one time, tventy years ago mit my son. Nutting dere; no shul, no cemetery. Nutting. I vent to see de house of my grandfadder. I vent to look at de house and all de neighbors came outside to look at me. I vas noivus. I left. Toidy minutes dere; maybe von hour. Nutting dere. My fadder vas born dere, 1900. He left in 1914, before de var. He vent to Romania. I vas born in Romania."

"Do you have anything, any pictures, writings, or stories, about Strzyzov in the late 1800s or early 1900s, Rabbi?" Out of the familiar, back to the formal.

"Vell . . ." A long pause, as if he was not sure he should reveal this next piece of information to me, a fellow whose Jewish bona fides he seriously doubted. "I haf a book."

"What kind of book?" My pulse quickened.

"*Seyfer Strzyzov.*"

"What's in the book?" This was sounding too good to be true.

"It's all about Strzyzov. How de people lived, about de rabbis, everyting up to de var, de second var, and it tells who died in de camps. Dere are pictures, too."

Bingo! I had just uncovered the mother lode.

"Can I see the book, Rabbi?"

"Can you read Hebrew?"

"No."

"Can you read Yiddish?"

"No."

"Vell, it's all in Hebrew and Yiddish." Case closed, as far as he was concerned.

For me, a momentary setback. Perhaps I could get it translated.

"Rebbe, can I come and sit with you for a while and talk about the old days and maybe take a look at the book?"

"Vhen do you vant to come?"

"Tomorrow."

"Let's see." Then a very long pause. "Okay. Tomorrow, five p.m."

The next day I struggled with what to bring the rabbi as a gesture of goodwill, an opening gambit. Food from my store—some lox and bagels, a few herrings, maybe some rugelach—would be a very welcome gift to most New Yorkers, but not to a *kashrut*-observant Orthodox Jew, and definitely not to a Hasidic rabbi. Even without stomach problems and diabetes, the Rebbe wouldn't eat the food from Russ & Daughters. My wife suggested some kosher wine. Good idea. So I stopped at our local wine shop and asked for the kosher wine section. The sales clerk needed to ask the manager, but they did have a small space on a small shelf in the back of the store with about five or six bottles of kosher wine. I spotted a Montepulciano, thinking it might be misplaced here, but the bottle's label clearly read "Kosher for Passover." This was great luck. I continued on to the rabbi's home in Borough Park, realizing about halfway there that I had forgotten to bring a head covering—either a hat or a yarmulke, a skullcap. The choice then became either to go back, get the hat, and be late for the rabbi, or to be on time but without a respectful head covering. This was a dilemma of Solomonic proportions, but cutting anything in half was not going to solve it. Then it occurred to me that the few times each year I go to my own synagogue there is always a box of skullcaps in the vestibule for those who prefer to wear one and have forgotten their own. In our Reform temple, head covering is optional. No doubt the rabbi would have extra yarmulkes available. My decision: Do not be late for the rabbi.

I arrived just on time at the rabbi's home, an apartment on the second floor of a three-story brick building. Attached to the building was a one-story annex that looked like it once might have been used as a dentist's office, but it now had a sign in Hebrew lettering that I couldn't read. But the bottom line was in English: STRZYZOVER SYNAGOGUE. I was in the right place. I was about to have an audience with a Hasidic rabbi, the Strzyzover Rebbe no less, who would, without a doubt, be a *tzaddik,* a holy man, the repository of the wisdom of the sages and, specifically, of all things Strzyzov. In the Hasidic tradition, the mantle of Rebbe is passed down from father to son (sometimes to son-in-law), from generation to generation. My expectation was that the Strzyzover Rebbe possessed the folklore and oral history of the Jews of Strzyzov, which he would have inherited from his father, who in turn would have inherited it from *his* father, et cetera, et cetera, going back who knows how many generations. And he would have The Book, the *Seyfer Strzyzov.* Perhaps he, or the book, would speak of the Russ family, my family, and their life in the Old Country. It was the Holy Grail I had been looking for. And here I was at the temple.

The rebbetzin greeted me at the door. Knowing that a Hasidic woman wouldn't shake hands with a man, I nodded my greeting. She led me into the kitchen and the rabbi immediately entered the room. He was a short man with a scraggly gray-white beard and *peyes* (sidelocks) tucked behind his ears. He wore black pants and laced-up shoes, white socks, a shirt buttoned to the neck (but no necktie), and a black brocade dressing gown. On his head was a large, round, wide-brimmed black felt hat. I was in the presence of a genuine *Chasidishe Rebbe.*

When I handed him the bottle of wine, the rabbi and his wife looked at the bottle briefly, then at each other, and then at me. You know how sometimes you bring someone a gift and they say "You shouldn't have" but they really mean "Thank you"? Well, it was pretty obvious to me that both the rabbi and the rebbetzin had a "You shouldn't have" look that *really meant* "You shouldn't have." No words were necessary, but it was clear that there was something wrong with bringing this bottle of wine into this house. Most likely its *kashrut* was certified by a rabbi whose authority was not recognized in the Hasidic world, but I did also have the slightly paranoid feeling that the very act of me, a nonreligious Jew, bringing the wine into this Hasidic home caused it somehow to transubstantiate, to go from kosher to non-kosher.

The rabbi escorted me into the dining room. As I took off my coat, he looked at my head and spoke his first words to me:

"Vhat, no hat?"

My apology was swift and sincere, and perhaps a bit stupid. "Rabbi, I'm terribly sorry. I mean no disrespect. I was running late when I remembered that I forgot a *kippa.* I don't usually wear a hat [that was the stupid part]. But if you have an extra *kippa,* I would be glad to put it on."

The rabbi didn't say anything, he just gave me a look. This look was easy to interpret: *Schmuck, it's too late to put on a hat now. The damage is done.*

He sat down at the head of the large dining table and motioned for me to sit next to him. Twelve people could sit comfortably around this table without adding any leaves to it. No doubt this is where the rabbi, when not in his shul, held court for visiting dignitaries or everyday suppliants. But it was doubtful that many *apikorsim* (Jews who are not traditional believers) like me would have spent time at this table.

At the other end of the room there was a wall unit containing three shelves of books and a desk. The books were all similarly bound, in two-toned black and yellowish-brown leather, with faded writing on the spines. These were Bibles, books of Jewish law, and other religious tracts. They all had the well-worn look of books that were in constant use. I was pretty sure that no murder mysteries, romance novels, or self-help books had ever been placed on these shelves.

I began by asking the rabbi questions about his background before moving on to the issue of The Book. He spoke of the family line of rabbis that preceded him. Apparently, in Strzyzov there were two feuding factions of Jews who were followers of two different but equally important rabbis; sometimes the feuds became violent. He was related to both sides of the feud, although I wasn't able to follow as he discussed all the branches on his family tree.

He was raised in Romania and survived World War II because the Jews in his area were not subjected to mass deportation and extermination by the Nazis. In 1944 the Soviet Army liberated Romania, but the Jews were not overly joyous because they had been taught to fear and hate the Russians. After the war, his family immigrated to Vienna, and from there went to the United States. Their first stop was Brownsville, Brooklyn, and then they moved to Borough Park.

I asked the rabbi if he had seen the documentary film called *The Jews of New York.* Perhaps knowing that the Russes were considered to be an important New York Jewish family by public television might put me in a favorable light. But the rabbi said he didn't have a television.

"You never watch television?" I asked.

"Vell, sometimes at de club," he said.

"What club?"

"De diamond dealers club."

I didn't get this at all. "You belong to a diamond dealers club?"

"Yes."

"Where?"

"Forty-seventh Street."

"Are you a diamond dealer?"

"Yes."

This was confusing news. "When were you a diamond dealer? Was it before you became a rabbi?"

"During de veek I sell diamonds; on de veekend I'm de rabbi." Talk about compartmentalizing.

As I mulled over this concept of dual careers, the rabbi walked over to the bookshelves, removed a very large black-brown tome, and brought it to the table. He opened it immediately, so I never got a chance to look at the cover. The pages appeared to be a parchment-type paper on which text that was either Hebrew or Yiddish was printed in double columns.

"*Seyfer Strzyzov!*" the rabbi declared, and with that he began reading. But he wasn't reading to me. He was reading to himself and swaying the way religious Jews do when praying—back and forth, with an occasional change in direction from side to side. He slowly leafed through the book, wetting his index finger as he turned the pages. He read with a great deal of focus, as if he had never studied this book before. He would interrupt his reading with the occasional "Aha!," which indicated recognition of something.

"What does it say, Rabbi?"

"It's all in here."

"What's in there?"

"Evryting. Evryting about Strzyzov. How de people lived. About de pogroms. About de rabbis. It's all here." There seemed to be something gloating in this response. He was teaching me a lesson: why it's necessary for a Jew, even in America, to read and speak Yiddish and Hebrew and, at the same time, why such a Jew should wear a skullcap and be careful about his choice of wines.

"Maybe I could have this book translated, Rabbi?" Here I tried my own version of a declaration phrased as a question. It didn't work.

"Too expensive."

"Maybe I could get someone to translate it for free."

He looked at me incredulously.

"Maybe YIVO will do it. Do you know about YIVO, Rabbi?" (YIVO is a New York–based institution focused on preserving the culture, history, and language of Eastern European Jews.)

"I hoid of dem."

"So maybe I can borrow the book and get it translated?"

"Foist find who'll do it. Den call me. Den we'll see." He wasn't letting this book out of his possession so fast.

About an hour and a half into this visit, I realized that I had gotten all I was going to get from the rabbi. It was time to go, but the rabbi seemed content to continue to read to himself. I would have to initiate the departure. Pushing away from the table, I rose three-quarters from my chair.

"Rabbi, I want to thank you for your time. I know you are a busy man, and you have been very generous to grant me this visit. I will not take up any more of your time."

He looked up from the book: "Vhere you going? Vhat's de rush? Siddown."

What would you do in the home of the Strzyzover Rebbe? I sat back down. He continued to read to himself.

Fifteen minutes passed, and then I heard the phone ring. The rebbetzin answered it and called to the rabbi in Yiddish.

"I haf a call from Israel," he said, by way of explanation. This was my opportunity to leave. It was obvious that I would be leaving without the book and without any more information from the rabbi. I had seen the Holy Grail, but its secrets were out of reach, encoded in Hebrew and Yiddish. The one who could decode it, the Strzyzover Rebbe, would not do so for me.

"Rabbi, you must take the call and I must get home. You have been overly generous with your time. I am grateful."

"Tank you fer a nice wisit."

The Lord works in mysterious ways. Or, at least, He works in ironical ways. Not more than two days after I visited the home of the Strzyzover Rebbe, I received an e-mail from a customer who is on the board of directors of the Jewish Genealogical Society. She had located a copy of *Seyfer Strzyzov* that had been translated into English at UCLA's

Charles E. Young Research Library. It was available only to students, faculty, and visiting scholars. Alas, I didn't fit into any of these categories. But my son the doctor was an assistant professor at UCLA Children's Hospital. Hoo-ha. On my next visit to him, I used his affiliation to borrow the English edition of the *Seyfer Strzyzov.*

Seyfer Strzyzov was assembled by Jews who once lived in Strzyzov and who avoided the Holocaust because they had the foresight to emigrate to Palestine or to the United States before the deportations began. The Strzyzover Rebbe was right when he told me that the book had "evryting. Evryting about Strzyzov." Chapter titles included "About the Rabbis in Strzyzov," "Strzyzov and Its Inhabitants," "About Daily Life and Trivial Events in Strzyzov," and "Personalities and Events." The subheadings—some sweetly comic, some heartbreakingly tragic—neatly summed up the stories that followed, about both ordinary life in a poor shtetl and the unimaginable horrors experienced by those who did and did not survive the war: "How Rabbi Chaim Halberstam from Sandz gave a thrashing to Reb Shlomo from Zyznow." "How Reb Yosl the sexton had suddenly gone deaf." "Every rabbi specializes in a different sickness." "Father said: 'Do not remain here!' " "Martydom and the sanctity of life."

Seyfer Strzyzow did contain references to "Russes" who lived in the town: Aryeh Leibush Russ; his wife, Rachel; and their three daughters, Sarah, Freda, and Roni (Ruth). Roni, a Zionist, immigrated to Palestine before the war and over the objection of her parents. She writes the following:

> *My father, Reb Aryeh Leibush Russ, and my mother, Rachel Yidis, were typical of the previous generation. They opposed my aliyah to Eretz Israel and I did it without their blessing. My dream to make aliyah materialized, but my happiness was mixed with sadness because I had to leave my parents when they had not yet recovered from the loss of their only son, Abraham. My brother, Abraham, died when he was only twenty-three years old. My sister Sarah with her husband, Moshe Blau, was planning to follow me. My brother-in-law was supposed to immigrate* [to Palestine] *as a rabbi, but the British Mandatory Government had cancelled the rabbinical privileges for aliyah and they, with their three children, remained in the foreign land. They were all annihilated by the Nazis, and I never merited to see them again. May G-d avenge their blood.*

I have never been able to determine whether we were related to these Russes. According to my mother and Aunt Hattie, Grandpa Russ had never mentioned any relatives in the Old Country; nor, come to think of it, did he ever even speak of the Holocaust. It was all part of the world he had left behind and was glad to forget. But how many Russes could there have been in the tiny shtetl of Strzyzov?

Although I've never been able to trace my family's roots in Strzyzov, the search did give me a wealth of information about our ancestral home, brought me to the home of the Strzyzover Rebbe in Borough Park, and to the *Seyfer Strzyzow* at UCLA. This itself was a unique experience that would now be passed down as part of the Russ family story.

Coming to America

With the help of Gail Adler, an amateur genealogist who offered to trade her investigative skills for smoked-sable sandwiches, I was able to piece together some historical facts: Grandpa Russ departed Hamburg, Germany, on January 8, 1907, and arrived at Ellis Island eleven days later. The ship was the *Kaiserin Auguste Victoria.* He traveled in *Zwischendeck* (steerage) and his occupation is given as *Bäckergeselle* (journeyman baker).

Joel Russ came to America at the age of twenty-one, when his eldest sister, Channah, sent for him. She lived with her husband, Isaac Ebbin, in a tenement on the Lower East Side, which was then one of the most densely populated places on earth. Grandpa Russ came, like every other immigrant, thinking he would find the *Goldeneh Medina,* the Golden Land. Although the streets weren't paved with gold, they were at least free from plundering, murderous Cossacks on horseback. And coming to America meant no longer having to worry about being conscripted into the Czar's army for twenty-five years, during which time, if you weren't killed in some war, all traces of your Jewish identity would be obliterated. Channah's sponsoring her brother Joel's immigration to America was a business decision as well as a display of family loyalty. Isaac Ebbin had established a herring business—or, more precisely, a

Joel Russ and his sister Channah Ebbin

herring stand—between two buildings on Hester Street. Herrings were fished out of large wooden barrels, wrapped in day-old newspapers, and sold to passersby on the street. Channah and Isaac had eight children. One day, Isaac decided to become a Talmudic scholar. The rigors of interpreting the word of God left Isaac no time for either selling herring or providing for his children. Channah was left to manage both.

The cost of sponsoring an immigrant in those days was twenty-five dollars. The price of a herring was a nickel. It took a lot of herring for Channah to bring Joel to the United States. Business was brisk for brother and sister, as herring was an inexpensive source of protein. A poor immigrant would take home and unwrap the herring, put it in a cast-iron skillet with some sliced potatoes and onions, and then

Isaac and Channah Ebbin

cook the dish in a coal-fired stove. With thick slices of black bread or rye or leftover Sabbath challah, this was a meal for an entire family. Those who lived in even more dire circumstances than the average poverty-stricken immigrant could make a single schmaltz herring last for two meals. For the first meal, the herring was rubbed on a piece of bread, leaving behind a layer of fat; the fish itself was saved for another meal.

Channah expanded her business by procuring a pushcart for Joel, which was set up not far from the Hester Street stall. She kept her brother's pushcart supplied with herring, and she kept an eye on the business as well.

By 1909, Joel had earned enough to pay back to his sister the twenty-five-dollar immigrant sponsorship fee. With his remaining profits he struck out on his own, starting with a visit to a matchmaker. He and Bella Spier, a simple peasant woman from the Galician shtetl of Skole, were married shortly thereafter. Their first child was a son, Morris, who died when he was a year and a half old, during the 1910 typhoid epidemic. Then came the three girls: Hattie in 1913, Ida in 1915, and my mother, Anne, in 1921. My grandparents' marriage lasted for almost fifty years. There must have been some sort of bond between them, but there were never any outward signs of love, or even tenderness. Until she died in 1959, Bella called her husband only by his last name, Russ, which she pronounced "Roos" in her heavy Eastern European accent. Joel called his wife Zug, which loosely translates from the Yiddish as "Hey, you."

Joel's first business was a candy store on Myrtle Avenue in Brooklyn, where he probably sold penny candies, cigarettes, Yiddish newspapers, and other sundries. A small candy store was one step up from

Grandma and Grandpa Russ with Aunt Hattie (left) and Aunt Ida, around 1920

a pushcart, even though this candy store was actually in a basement, below street level. Candy shops proliferated in poor neighborhoods because the initial capital investment was modest. Grandpa Russ sold it after four years and used the proceeds to open his first appetizing store, Russ's Cut Rate Appetizing, at 187 Orchard Street. It was back to the Lower East Side.

So, What's an Appetizing Store?

Push open the door at Russ & Daughters and the first thing to hit you is the store's unique aroma. It's a combination of smokiness from whitefish, salmon, sturgeon, and sable; the brininess of herrings and pickles; the yeastiness of freshly baked bagels and bialys; and the sweetness of rugelach, babka, chocolates, and halvah. How I wish I could bottle that singular scent—smoky, briny, yeasty, and sweet.

It's important, for historical reasons, to say what an appetizing store is not. It is not a deli. Appetizing stores came into being as the anti-deli. The laws of *kashrut* prohibit cooking and eating dairy and meat products together. To make sure that these laws are observed, kosher delis prepare and sell cured, smoked, and pickled meat—pastrami, salami, bologna, tongue, frankfurters, and corned beef—under the supervision of a *mashgiach,* a rabbi trained in the intricacies of these dietary laws. Because smoked fish is traditionally eaten with butter or cream cheese on bagels or bread, and because herring is often covered with cream sauce, these products needed a store of their own if they were to have rabbinical supervision. Thus was born the appetizing store. Added to the mix is the American phenomenon of "kosher style," which describes delis without rabbinical supervision that also sell dairy products, such as cheese blintzes, and appetizing stores without rabbinical supervision that sell both kosher and non-kosher fish, such as sturgeon. Russ & Daughters has always been a kosher-style appetizing store. Grandpa Russ left his orthodoxy in the Old Country.

The word "appetizing," as in "appetizing store," has no known foreign origin. Stores specializing in smoked, cured, and pickled fish did not exist in Eastern Europe. The local fishmonger sold pike and carp for the Sabbath and salt herring for during the week; housewives took it from there. In America, newly available fish, such as whitefish, sable, and salmon—which along with the familiar herring lent themselves to smoking, curing, and pickling—gave rise to a new type of establishment: the "appetizing store," where mouthwatering ("appetizing") prepared food was sold.

Delicatessens, on the other hand, did make the journey from Old World to New World. Germans, who settled on the Lower East Side in the mid-1800s, brought the delicatessen concept with them. The neighborhood was even known for a time as Kleine Deutschland (Little Germany). But before long these upwardly mobile merchants and tradesman moved their community to the Upper East Side, beating a quick retreat before the onslaught of the "wretched refuse" that were the Eastern European Jews. That was okay with the new immigrants, so long as the delicatessens, under different ownership, stayed in the neighborhood.

From the 1920s through the end of World War II, there were twenty to thirty appetizing stores on the Lower East Side. Many owners shared Grandpa Russ's career trajectory—from pushcart to store. But none that I know of, save for Russ & Daughters, made it past the second generation. They weren't designed to. No one wanted their kids in the business.

Russ's Cut Rate Appetizing

I recently asked Aunt Hattie if she remembered anything of her father's first store at 187 Orchard Street. "Do you know," I asked, "why your father called it Cut Rate Appetizing?"

"I can't imagine," replied Aunt Hattie. "There were lots of appetizing stores on the Lower East Side. And prices were cheap as borscht. Maybe lox was seven or eight cents a quarter pound. And no one bought a quarter pound, anyway. They bought a *halbe fiertel* [an eighth of a pound]. So I don't know what rate they could cut. A lot of the customers did try to bargain, but Papa wouldn't allow it. He posted the prices, and that's what they paid. Papa never did well with the customers.

"Papa opened the store in 1914. It was very dark. It was very small. No refrigeration. There were wooden herring barrels outside. I don't know how they got there every day. We lived in one room in the back of the store. When my sister Ida was born, we moved to an apartment in the tenement across the street. We walked up to the fourth floor. It was very dark. It was very hot in the summer. We spent a lot of time on the fire escape to stay cool. The bathroom was in the hallway. The bathtub was in the kitchen.

"I started helping Papa in the store on weekends when I was eight years old. I have a memory of Papa having a horse and wagon. Maybe he had used it for deliveries. I remember sitting up on the wagon with him. But I don't know where he got the horse and wagon from, where he kept it, or what he did with it."

Berger's Amphibious Steed

Grandpa Russ bought the store in 1914 from the previous owner, Isaac Berger. In *The New York Times* of September 11, 1911, there's a story titled "Berger's Amphibious Steed." According to the *Times,* one Isaac Berger owned a smoked-fish business at 187 Orchard Street and a horse named Chestnut. All winter long, Berger and Chestnut would deliver smoked fish to East Side customers. "Then when summer came," the article recounts,

> Chestnut together with the other members of the Berger family went splendidly to the seashore and sniffed the cool and restful breezes of the ocean when he faced it, and of smoked fish when he faced the other way. For Berger mingles business with pleasure and opened a summer trade in smoked fish at 526 Boulevard, Rockaway Beach.
>
> The brightest hour in Chestnut's life at the seashore and the proudest in Berger's was at four o'clock each afternoon, when, leaving smoked fish and business cares on shore behind them, both swam out into the surf. Berger was the only one of all the bathers who had the proud distinction of breasting the waves with a dashing steed.

"Aunt Hattie," I asked, "do you remember the name of the horse your father had?"

"No."

"Does the name Chestnut mean anything to you?"

"No."

"Did you ever hear your father mention a horse that swims?"

"What, are you crazy? A horse that swims? Whoever heard such a thing?"

Moving the Store and the Family

In 1923 Joel Russ moved his store around the corner to 179 East Houston Street. This location had been a storage space that Grandpa Russ shared with Hagel, his *landsman* (someone from the same area in Europe) and partner in the imported-mushroom business. Dried mushrooms from Poland were a staple in those days. They had a rich, earthy taste and were used in soups and sauces instead of meat, which was too expensive for many tenement dwellers. Due to a falling out between the two men, Grandpa Russ was able to take over the space and open J. Russ Cut Rate Appetizing. It was a small store, on one side of the street level of a six-story tenement building, no more than sixteen feet wide and forty feet deep. There were floor-to-ceiling sliding glass doors that made the store unbearably hot in the summer and freezing cold in the winter. When the weather was good, the doors were removed and the large wooden herring barrels were dragged from the back of the store out to the street. There was no bathroom in the store; it was located in the hallway of the residential part of the building. Sheets of newspaper were left to be used as toilet paper.

The Lower East Side of the 1920s was crowded, dirty, and poor, and the mostly Jewish and Italian immigrants left as soon as they earned enough money to live in the newly constructed apartment buildings and houses in Brooklyn, Queens, and the Bronx. The period after World War I was one of economic expansion for the city. The subway system now linked Brooklyn, the Bronx, and Queens with Manhattan, making the outer boroughs ideal areas for families to live, while the family breadwinners commuted to the jobs and businesses they kept on the Lower East Side.

Street scene in front of 179 East Houston Street (on the left, in the foreground) in 1929, looking toward First Avenue

Grandpa Russ joined that exodus. There were short-lived forays into Williamsburg, Brooklyn, and Corona, Queens. But in 1926 he was able to move his wife and daughters to a two-family house at 715 Avenue O, in the Flatbush/Midwood section of Brooklyn. He had to take out two mortgages. Grandma Russ finally embraced life in America. She had two kitchens—one for baking, the other for cooking—and a large garden where she grew flowers and vegetables. The Russ girls were happy because each had her own room, attended good schools, and made new friends. My mother even had some boyfriends. And Grandpa Russ was happy. He had *landsleit* in the neighborhood, two cronies from Strzyzov who frequently came over on Friday nights to laugh and tell stories. And one day he brought home a German shepherd named Buddy, to whom he told jokes in Yiddish. He swore that the dog laughed at his jokes.

Living in Brooklyn meant Grandpa Russ had to leave the house at 3:30 every morning to go by foot, trolley car, and BMT elevated subway line first to the smokehouses and then to his store. He had very bad feet. He would say, "*Fees, oyb de kinst nisht, ubba ich loz dich du*" (Feet, if you're not coming, I'll leave you here). But he knew that living in Brooklyn was better for his family.

Vi Nempt Men Parnosa?

One day in 1932, in the middle of the Great Depression, two representatives from the banks that held the two mortgages on the Brooklyn house came to visit Grandpa Russ.

"Mr. Russ," they said, "your store or your house?"

Grandpa Russ chose to keep the store. His wife and daughters pleaded with him; they were happy in Brooklyn and didn't want to return to the Lower East Side. He replied with what had become his constant refrain: "*Vi nempt men parnosa?*" From where do we take our living? He meant that it was more important to hold on to the store because that was the source of the family's income.

The five Russes moved to a dark, dreary ground-floor apartment complete with cockroaches in a tenement on Second Street and Avenue A. But they didn't stay there for long, thanks to Cousin Sylvia, daughter of Tante Pepe, Bella's sister. Bella and Pepe didn't get along and rarely spoke to each other, even though they lived just a few blocks apart. According to my mom, it was jealousy, pure and simple. Bella married Joel, who had his own store and his daughters in the business. Pepe married a barber. But the barber was able to use his connections—his customers—to get his children good civil-service jobs, which was no easy feat during the Depression. Cousin Sylvia worked for the Board of Health, and she was able to have the Russes' apartment condemned for roach infestation, allowing Grandpa Russ to break the lease.

He then moved the family to the Ageloff Towers. Completed in 1929, the Ageloff was marketed at the time as "the Lower East Side's first luxury building." And indeed it was. Covering the entire block from Third to Fourth Streets on Avenue A, the two twelve-story apartment houses were built in art-deco style, which was then the height of architectural fashion. They offered "all modern conveniences," including doormen with white gloves, elevators, both hot and cold running water, and indoor plumbing, all in sharp contrast to the surrounding cold-water six-story walk-up tenements. The offering brochure also touted the multitude of transportation alternatives: "At the door are the 14th Street and 8th Street Crosstown Street Cars. Nearby are the Interborough, the B.M.T., the Second and Third Avenue Elevated . . ." But the availability of transportation was not critical to Grandpa Russ. He and the rest of the Russes simply walked the few blocks to the store. But then a new problem arose. The Second Avenue elevated line was dismantled, and the street right in front of the store underwent a massive excavation to create the new Independent Subway Line. The work lasted for several years, and the hardship it created for all the businesses on East Houston Street was worse than the problems brought on by the Depression. It was almost impossible to get people or merchandise into the store. I was curious about how Grandpa Russ could afford to move the family into such a fancy building at the height of the Depression and in the middle of the East Houston Street excavation. My mother provided the answer.

"We all lived in the five-room apartment," she said. "Mama and Papa had one bedroom. Ida and her husband, Max, and their new baby, Lolly, were in another. Hattie and Murray and their new baby, Nina, used the living room as their bedroom. And I slept in the dining room with the maids."

"You had maids?" I was shocked to hear this. It didn't fit in with the image of my struggling immigrant family of fishmongers.

"Sure. Hattie and Ida were working full-time in the store with their husbands. I was going to Seward Park High School. Mama's spirit and health had been broken by the move from the big house in Brooklyn back to the Lower East Side. Mama needed help with the babies, and with the cleaning and shopping. One maid was from Czechoslovakia. She didn't speak any English, but Mama could communicate with her in some Slavic language. The other maid was from somewhere in the South. She spoke English, but none of us could understand her. And do you know what they got paid? Fifteen dollars a month! It was *bilik vee borscht* [cheap as borscht]. They were happy to have jobs, food, and a roof over their heads."

The Pushcart Wars

The 1930s were a time of transition on the Lower East Side. When Mayor Fiorello La Guardia was elected in 1933, there were thousands of pushcarts in the neighborhood, selling everything from clothes to food to housewares. The mayor saw them as unsightly reminders of Old World living, and all the human traffic they brought with them made it difficult for police cars and fire trucks to get through the crowded streets. With federal money given to the city for job creation, La Guardia built several clean indoor markets throughout the city. The Essex Street Market at Essex and Delancey Streets opened in 1940 to house the pushcart vendors from Orchard Street, Hester Street, and the surrounding areas of the Lower East Side.

The pushcart controversy hit home. Grandma Russ loved to shop from the pushcarts in the streets, while Grandpa Russ organized with other storekeepers to modernize the neighborhood and push out the pushcarts. When Grandma Russ reminded Grandpa that he had once been a pushcart peddler himself, he said, very simply, "*Sha!*" (Be quiet!).

One by one, the Russ girls, all of whom had helped their father in his store on weekends, came to work there full-time, six days a week, as soon as they finished high school. After all, it was the Depression. *Vi nempt men parnosa?* Although Hattie, Ida, and Anne resented the loss of their youth, they also recognized the economic necessity. And their father recognized that they were good for business. He was a typical Eastern European immigrant, long on drive and short on patience, especially with customers. This was not a good attitude to have in retail. But the three young and pretty Russ daughters, with their arms up to their elbows in herring barrels or their hands deftly slicing lox, were able to charm and disarm the most difficult customer.

By 1935, with two of his daughters running his business right alongside him and the third soon to follow, Joel Russ renamed his store Russ & Daughters. Joel Russ wasn't a feminist, but he recognized two

Joel Russ and his daughters (left to right), Hattie, Ida, and Anne

things: first, that it was indeed his daughters who had helped him grow his business and keep his store; second, that the name Russ & Daughters would be a good marketing tool. Of the twenty or so other appetizing shops in the neighborhood, some were "So-and-So & Sons." Only Joel Russ had a sign that read "& Daughters." When his daughters married, their husbands worked in the store, too, and eventually became legal partners in the business. But the sign would never be changed.

The War: Good for Business

During World War II, Hattie's husband, Murray, and Ida's husband, Max, both avoided the draft. I never found out how; my aunts never said. My father, Herbie, was drafted into the U.S. Navy, where he was designated "Storekeeper 3rd Class," a bit of ethnic typecasting by a navy that at the time was regarded by many as anti-Semitic. Herbie had thought he would be escaping, at least temporarily, from the world behind the counter. No such luck. But this may have saved his life. He was never shipped overseas. He eventually wound up in New Orleans, and then he was stationed in Texas. My mother went with him, and they were thankful for the hospitality of local Jewish families during

Anne and Storekeeper 3rd Class Herbert Federman

holidays. My mother says the best challah she ever ate was in Fort Worth, Texas.

Business boomed for Russ & Daughters during the war years. Due to rationing, it was difficult to obtain canned goods, but Grandpa Russ, ever resourceful, was able to procure canned tuna, salmon, and sardines. Customers knew that Mr. Russ had the merchandise. They entered the store, spoke quietly to Grandpa or Uncle Murray, and then were directed around the corner to a small warehouse. Customers pulled up in front of the warehouse, opened their car trunks, and cases were loaded directly into them. I was told by Aunt Hattie that some of the biggest customers ("doctors, lawyers, and even judges") were buying Grandpa Russ's black-market sardines.

Since the canned-goods business proved such a success, Grandpa and Uncle Murray headed to Maine, where they purchased a carload—a train carload—of Moosabec sardines, a well-known brand back then. But their timing was off. Soon after they took delivery, the war ended, and canned goods were once again readily available. The sardines stayed "on special, three for a quarter" for years. When I renovated the store in 1995, a thorough clearing of the basement unearthed eight cases of Moosabec sardines dated 1945. The cans were all swollen. They went into a Dumpster.

The Postwar Years

The period following World War II was one of great economic expansion in the United States, and the Russ family fully participated. While Grandpa Russ kept everyone working together in the store on the Lower East Side, he also joined the exodus from inner city to suburb and moved the entire family to Far Rockaway, Queens. The Russes had rented bungalows by the beach for several summers during the 1940s, but the move became permanent in 1949. Grandpa Russ bought a big old two-story wood-frame house that contained two apartments—without telling anyone beforehand. He never told his family where or when the next move would be. "Papa had made up his mind," the saying went. "*Shoyn. Fartig*" (That's it. Decided).

Grandpa Russ, in an uncharacteristic display of affection, and me, in front of one of the Hudson Commodores, sometime in the early 1950s. Maybe he knew he was anointing the heir to the herring throne.

My family lived on the first floor; Aunt Hattie, Uncle Murray, and their two kids, Nina and Paul, lived on the second floor. Grandpa and Grandma Russ occupied a cute red-shingled cottage next door. Aunt Ida and Uncle Max had left the business that year to strike out on their own in the world of appetizing. They moved to Far Rockaway, too, just a few blocks away from the family compound, with their two kids, Lolly and Martin.

Life in the suburbs was safer and easier for the third generation. My sisters, cousins, and I walked to public schools, rode our bikes to the beach, and played in the streets. But for Grandpa Russ and our parents, it meant commuting to the city to work, a forty-five-minute drive "in good weather with no traffic." One of the few perks of being in the family business was getting to buy a new car every three years. My father and Uncle Murray always chose the same American-made car, but in different colors, starting with Hudson Commodores in 1950 and then switching to Chryslers. Big cars with big trunks could hold many boxes of fish on the days when the store's truck broke down.

When stops at the smokehouses were necessary to pick up fish for the store, the commute to Manhattan began at 6:00 a.m. The store opened for business at 9:00 a.m. and closed at 7:00 p.m. On Saturdays during the 1930s, '40s, and '50s, we opened at 8:00 a.m. and stayed open until one or two in the morning to capture the crowd just coming out of the many Yiddish theaters along nearby Second Avenue, which was known as the Jewish Rialto. Sometimes the great actors themselves would come in to pick up a late-night snack or fixings for a Sunday brunch: Molly Picon, Menasha Skulnik, Aaron Lebedeff, and Jennie Goldstein were all regulars, the rock stars of our world in their day.

By the 1960s, when the Yiddish theaters on the Lower East Side were a thing of the past, the store closed at 10:00 p.m. on Saturday nights. By then there were two daughters and their husbands running the business, and they divided the long days into manageable shifts of ten hours each.

The store was closed on Tuesdays. Tuesday was our Shabbos. All family functions—weddings, birthday parties, bar and bat mitzvahs—had to be scheduled for Tuesdays. Death, of course, could not be planned, and so funerals were exempt from the Tuesday rule. Vacation times were also set in stone. The store was closed during Passover, because bagels—the most popular accompaniment to smoked fish—cannot be eaten during the eight-day holiday. And it was closed for two weeks during the summer, when everyone tried to escape the city's oppressive heat.

Whatever Jewish life and commerce managed to survive on the Lower East Side through the 1970s slowly began to disappear in the 1980s, hastened by the repeal of the Sunday blue laws (retail stores such as Macy's and Gimbels weren't legally allowed to be open on Sundays until the 1970s, but stores on the Lower East Side were exempt from this law) and the advent of suburban malls. Consumers, particularly nostalgic Jewish consumers, no longer drove into Manhattan from Long Island or New Jersey to shop for bargains on Sundays. The Orchard Street shops that once teemed with customers lining up to buy discount designer dresses, men's suits in large and portly sizes, brassieres and undergarments at half price, the latest shoes and handbags from Italy, and socks and underpants—by the dozen only—were often empty. As the immigrant and first-generation Jews who founded these shops grew older, they followed their customers to the suburbs or closed their businesses altogether and moved to Florida.

But then something interesting began to happen. Writers, artists, and musicians started moving into the neighborhood, attracted by the cheap rents and the "energy" of a neighborhood in economic and social free fall. Sometimes they would come into the store to buy some dried fruit or a bagel; they weren't rich or famous enough yet to afford the lox. That would come later.

City services also abandoned the Lower East Side. The successive waves of Hispanic and Asian immigrants who now inhabited the tenements of the Lower East Side found their buildings painted with graffiti and their dirty streets populated by drug addicts, prostitutes, and petty thieves. The shops that did remain in business adopted a siege mentality. Stores were shuttered each night with roll-up gates made of solid sheets of metal. Russ & Daughters was one of the few shops that kept its old-fashioned latticework gates so pedestrians could view the merchandise. The family's reasoning was simple: Who would want to break into a shop that sells fish? But, as extra insurance, my parents and uncle and aunt made a habit of inviting the cops on the beat to have bagel-and-lox lunches in the back of the store, hoping that this would result in our benefiting from a little more "protection."

Aunt Hattie and Uncle Murray intended to retire in 1975. They had put their entire lives into the store and they were tired. Though Murray was slipping just a bit, they were in sufficiently good health to enjoy the remainder of their lives in Florida, where Murray would become the shuffleboard champion of Bal Harbor and Hattie would become the president of the local ORT (a Jewish charitable organization). But they had to put off retirement for one more year to cover the store while my father recovered from his seventh heart attack. As is often said in the Russ family, "*A mentsch tracht und Gott lacht*" (Man plans and God laughs).

And then, in 1978, to the astonishment of everyone, I left a job at a highly regarded uptown law firm to sell herring and smoked fish on the Lower East Side. You could say I went from Lex to lox. But more about that later. First, meet the rest of the family.

Mushroom Barley Soup

MAKES 6 TO 8 SERVINGS

½ ounce dried Polish mushrooms or dried porcini mushrooms*
6 tablespoons unsalted butter
1 medium onion, diced
3 cloves garlic, minced
¾ pound fresh mushrooms, trimmed and thinly sliced
2 stalks celery with leaves, diced
1 large carrot, peeled and diced
¼ cup chopped fresh parsley
1 tablespoon all-purpose flour
1 quart low-sodium beef broth
¾ cup barley, rinsed
2 teaspoons kosher salt
Freshly ground black pepper

Put the dried mushrooms in a bowl and cover them with 2 cups of boiling water. Allow them to soak for 1 hour. Strain the mushrooms through a cheesecloth-lined sieve into a bowl. Reserve the liquid. Coarsely chop the mushrooms and set aside.

Melt the butter in a large, heavy stockpot or Dutch oven over medium-high heat. Add the onions and sauté until softened and translucent, about 8 minutes. Add the garlic and sauté until fragrant, about 2 minutes more. Add the fresh mushrooms, celery, carrot, and half of the parsley, and sauté until the mushrooms are golden and the celery and carrots are beginning to soften, about 10 minutes. Stir in the flour until well blended. Stir in the mushroom soaking liquid, soaked mushrooms, beef broth, and 4 cups of water. Stir in the barley, salt, and pepper to taste.

Bring the mixture to a boil, stirring frequently. Reduce the heat to low and simmer until the barley is tender, about 30 to 40 minutes. If the soup is too thick, add a little more water. Adjust the seasoning with more salt and pepper if necessary. Sprinkle with the remaining parsley before serving.

**Using a blend of fresh mushrooms is also nice. Try shiitake, cremini, or button.*

2

The Family

Growing Up Fishy

Medical benefits, 401(k)s, and vacation and sick days were unheard-of during the early years at Russ & Daughters. There was no such thing as a human resources department to hire and fire employees. For Joel Russ, his family was his labor pool. And it was pretty cheap labor at that. In 1935 Grandpa Russ paid Hattie and Murray twenty-five dollars a week. For both of them. He paid the same salary to Ida and Max. Anne was still in high school then and worked only on weekends. She knew better than to ask for a salary for her work. She wouldn't have gotten one.

The Wife

Grandma Russ was Grandpa's first employee. Grandma's style of dealing with customers was the opposite of her husband's. At the slightest hint that a customer might be difficult, Grandpa Russ would say, "*Rebbetzin, tog mir a toyveh, fahrlir mein ahdres*" (Lady, do me a favor, lose my address), first in Yiddish and then English. Grandma Russ, on the other hand, would say only, "*Vifil kimpt mir?*" (How much do you owe me?). She had a heart of gold and would do anything to please a customer. But she couldn't read, write, or add up a column of figures, so she had to ask the customers to tell her the price of each item, to calculate the total, and to count out the change she owed them. Needless to say, her employment at the store was short-lived; she soon went back to cleaning their tenement apartment, shopping from the pushcart peddlers, and caring for her family.

Grandma and Grandpa Russ

The Brother

When Joel Russ's older brother Shmemendel (the name is a combination of his first name, Shmuel, and his second name, Mendel) arrived from Poland in 1921, he needed a job. Grandpa Russ needed help in the store, so he hired his brother.

Shmemendel was a very religious Jew. Like many Eastern European Jewish immigrants, he brought the shtetl ways and his religious practices and beliefs with him to America. He wore a black Hasidic caftan, had a long beard and *peyes* (sidelocks), and spoke only Yiddish. He kept strictly kosher.

Shmemendel's brother Joel (known as Yoi'el back in Poland) wore American-style clothing and taught himself to read and write English. Joel kept a kosher home because his wife insisted on it, but he ate *trayfe* outside the house and sold non-kosher sturgeon in his store, which he kept open on the Sabbath to cater to other nonreligious Lower East Side Jewish families who wanted to buy fish on Saturdays. Joel gave

Grandpa Russ and Uncle Shmemendel

up the shtetl way of life as soon as he stepped on American soil. He referred to his brother and other Orthodox Jews as *fanatishe chnyuks*—over-the-top religious fanatics.

Because he was Orthodox, Shmemendel refused to work on the Sabbath. But that wasn't what got him fired. It was more a matter of his unique ideas about customer service. When customers came into the store, Shmemendel would say to them in Yiddish, "Why do you want to shop here? Don't you know this store isn't kosher?" When Joel found out about this, Uncle Shmemendel was gone the next day. He moved to Brooklyn and became the sexton in an Orthodox synagogue. Grandpa Russ and the rest of the family had almost nothing to do with him after that. Shmemendel occasionally showed up at the store, looking for "some help for the shul" from his brother, which he always got.

While researching this book, I found Shmemendel Russ's descendants living in Borough Park. Shmemendel's great-grandson David heard that I was writing a book about the Russ family and wanted his side of the story included. "If you're gonna write about the irreligious Russes," David said, "you should mention the religious ones, too." He then told me a story that has become part of his side of the Russ family's oral history: "Yoi'el Russ had one barrel of herring. All day long he would stand in front of that barrel. When someone came along and asked for a schmaltz herring, he would turn around and pick a herring from the front of the barrel. If someone asked for a matjes herring, he would turn around and pick from the back of the barrel. And from one barrel of herring Yoi'el Russ *macht a lebn* [made a living]!"

The Nephew

Aaron "Ari" Ebbin, son of Grandpa Russ's sister Channah, was the next relative to be offered the opportunity to earn a living in Joel's store. One day, Joel accused his nephew of stealing the day's cash receipts instead of taking them to the bank. Highly insulted, Aaron quit. The money was found a week later on one of the store's shelves in a brown paper bag behind the jumbo ripe olives. Just where Joel had left it. Joel didn't apologize—it was not in his nature—but he did ask Aaron to come back to work. Channah, though, stepped in and said no. Her son couldn't work for someone—especially an uncle—who thought he was a thief! Some years later, when Aaron wanted to set up an auto-wrecking business on Staten Island, he asked his uncle Joel for a loan. Joel thought it was a good investment opportunity and offered to put up the money in return for part ownership in the business. Aaron said there was no way they could be partners after he had been accused of being a thief. And so Aaron got the money someplace else and established a successful auto-wrecking company, which eventually became much more profitable than his uncle's fish store. Aaron came to regard the "stealing" incident as a blessing in disguise; it got him out of the Lower East Side and out of the fish business.

The Daughters and Their Husbands

Grandpa Russ was running out of relatives. Then it occurred to him to look closer to home. Hattie, his oldest daughter, started to help out in the store on weekends when she was eight years old. Almost immediately, Grandpa realized that he was onto something here. Unlike her mother, Hattie could read, write, and make change. And although she spoke not a word of English until she entered public school, by the time she was eight she was fluent in her new language. When she was sixteen, Hattie dropped out of school to work in the store full-time. It was 1929, the stock market had just crashed, and the Great Depression had begun. Until then the store had been doing well, but the failing economy began to take its toll, business slowed down, and Hattie was needed only on weekends.

In the Old Country, Grandpa had been apprenticed to a shoemaker at the age of nine, then to a baker. If he was sent out to earn money for the family, he figured his daughter should do the same. Hattie, the dutiful Russ daughter, never questioned her father. It was always "Yes, Papa." Hattie's first job was with Wildfeuer Brothers Shoes. They had six stores, including two on the Lower East Side, but Hattie applied for and got a job in the fancy-schmancy flagship store on Fifth Avenue and Forty-fourth Street, where, she reported, "all the big people shopped, even Clara Bow." She kept the books, took stenography in the office upstairs, and, when needed, modeled shoes in the store. She was a perfect size 4B. Occasionally, the owners sent her a few blocks away to I. Miller on Forty-second Street to buy a pair of shoes, to "see what's doing at the competition." Hattie fit right in at Wildfeuer; she was always impeccably dressed for work and wore fashionably high heels in spite of the long walk from home to the subway. According to her baby sister, Anne, Hattie always looked "like she stepped out of a bandbox." But family was family, after all, and Hattie continued to sell lox and herring for her father on the weekends. And in 1932, when Wildfeuer went bankrupt, Hattie went back to work in the store full-time.

But shoes continued to play a major role in Hattie's life. While shopping with Ida one day at A. S. Beck, Hattie met Murray Gold, a shoe salesman who fell in love with her perfect size 4Bs. The deal

Hattie and Murray Gold

was sealed when Murray found out that Hattie's mother made gefilte fish "on the sweet side." He, like the Russes, was a Galitzianer, and his food preferences tended toward the sweet rather than the salt and pepper of the Litvaks. Galitzianers came from southern Poland and the western Ukraine; Litvaks came from Lithuania and northern Poland. As if Eastern European Jews didn't have it bad enough, what with the ever-present threat of pogroms orchestrated by the neighboring gentiles, these two groups became the shtetl version of the Hatfields and the McCoys. Litvaks were considered more intellectual and studious; Galitzianers were thought of as more spiritual and emotional. Each ridiculed and looked down on the other. And according to the Litvaks, one of the worst things about Galitzianers was that they put sugar in *everything*—including, heaven help us, gefilte fish.

Murray's interest in Hattie, plus the anticipation of sweet gefilte fish, emboldened him to invite himself over for dinner one Friday night. Envisioning how good Murray would look behind the fish counter (he was said to look "just like the actor Brian Donlevy") and appreciating his experience in retail, Grandpa Russ approved of the match. Murray and Hattie married in 1935, a few months after they had met, and Murray became Grandpa Russ's newest employee. In the beginning, Murray found the early-morning trips to the smokehouses difficult; after all, shoe stores didn't open until 10:00 a.m. But Murray eventually got used to the hours and, after her second child was born, Hattie was finally able to "take it easy." Which is to say that she had to work in the store only on weekends and holidays.

When I was a kid working on the candy side of the store in the 1950s, I would watch Hattie handle the customers on the fish side. I have never seen anything quite like it. She was short—maybe five feet tall—and could barely see over the high counters. But her voice traveled easily enough, conveying a combination of pride in her product and regret over each piece of fish she sold, as if it were a child about to be given up for adoption. When the customer begged for a particular piece of fish, Hattie would give it up only with the greatest reluctance ("Mrs. Feigenbaum, this is the prettiest fish I've seen in years. I hate to part with it."). After I took over the store in 1978 and was the only Russ working the counter, I tried several styles of salesmanship, includ-

Ida, Grandpa Russ, Hattie, Grandma Russ, and Anne at Hattie's wedding

ing Aunt Hattie's. One day, I held up a particularly fat whitefish for a particularly old and difficult customer, saying, "Have you ever seen such a beautiful fish? This is the fish I should take home to my family." Whereupon the customer replied, "Listen, son, do us both a favor. You take it home. And let me give you a piece of advice: Don't fall in love with the inventory."

Ida and Max

Ida was born in the back of the Orchard Street store in 1915. When the back room that housed Joel, Bella, Hattie, and the herring barrels became too small, Joel moved his family across the street. There was no hot running water in the family's fourth-floor walk-up, but at least it had two rooms.

Ida was a handful from the start. Hattie recalls, "There were lots of pushcarts and people on Orchard Street; you could hardly move. Sometimes Ida would run up to the roof and I had to go look for her. I told her that it was dangerous to run away. But nothing scared Ida. She jumped up and down on the bed until it broke and then blamed me. I was a year and a half older and in charge of her."

Even her stern and strict papa found it difficult to control Ida. She argued with him about everything and anything; no one else dared to.

Ida and Max

She began working in the store on weekends when she was twelve years old, and then became a full-time employee after graduating from Lincoln High School in Brooklyn. It wasn't as though she had any other options. It was 1932; jobs were still scarce, and Grandpa Russ needed help in the store. College was out of the question. Getting married appeared to be the only way out for Ida. Less than a year after Hattie married Murray, Ida married Maxie Pulvers, who seemed to be a young man with potential. He had his own business, a luncheonette. But Max's business was in even worse shape than Grandpa Russ's, and so he also wound up working for his father-in-law. And he and Ida moved with the rest of the Russ family into the two-bedroom apartment in the Ageloff Towers.

But there was soon trouble in paradise. Neither Grandpa Russ nor Uncle Murray could abide Uncle Max, who had the habit of getting lost for hours—and sometimes for days—when making deliveries of herring and lox. Apparently the feeling was mutual. The story goes that one day Max was driving the store's truck in a heavy rainstorm, saw his father-in-law walking in the rain, and didn't stop to pick him up. The other family members never forgot this slight. By 1950 Max and Ida no longer worked at Russ & Daughters. Whether they quit or were fired remains a family mystery to this day. Ida went to work at the appetizing counter of a supermarket, then had a stand on the weekends in a farmers' market on Long Island, where she and Max sold herring and smoked fish. Ida eventually opened her own appetizing store, proud of the quality of her fish and her heritage as one of the Russ daughters from the Lower East Side. Several years later Ida and Max divorced. In those days divorce was something of a scandal in a Jewish family. But in this case, everyone thought "it was for the best." Her second marriage, to Louis Schwartz, was much happier.

Even with business and marital difficulties, Ida always stayed in touch with her sisters and her parents. There was never much time for a visit; everyone worked in retail. But by the 1990s the three Russ daughters, now retired and widowed, moved into the same gated community in Florida. Anne, the youngest, did the driving at night. Ida had the best palate and determined where they would eat. And Hattie, the eldest, kept the peace.

Anne and Herbie

Born in 1921, the youngest of the Russ daughters, Anne was happy living in the big house on Avenue O in Brooklyn. She had lots of friends, and by age ten, even a boyfriend. Except for weekend shopping trips with her mother to the pushcart vendors of Orchard Street, she wasn't as familiar with the Lower East Side as her older sisters were. She enjoyed the trips by trolley and train, even if her mother embarrassed her by talking to anyone and everyone in her heavy Eastern European accent. "Those who were not that familiar with Jews," she told me, "thought that Mama was speaking Italian. In our big house in Brooklyn, Mama finally seemed to be happy in America. She loved to grow things in her garden and would buy plants every week from the man who drove by in his horse and wagon. Sometimes on Saturdays she would take me with her to the movies and the five-and-dime."

Anne least understood and most resented the move back to the Lower East Side, the move that "broke the heart and the spirit of Mama." The economic depression that had engulfed the world was taking its personal toll on the Russ household as well; Mama's long disappearances into her room would be attributed to "high blood pressure" by the family, but everyone knew what was really behind them.

At age fourteen, Anne began working in the store on weekends. And following the path that her papa had laid down for her sisters, once she graduated from Seward Park High School (her classmate Walter Matthau once walked her home and carried her books), she began working in the store full-time. But it was different for Anne than it had been for Hattie and Ida. The baby of the family was now an employee with five supervisors: her father, her sisters, and their husbands. She was not happy. No one saw her as a teenager with a life of her own; she was just cheap labor. But Anne never complained, although she resented the ten-to-twelve-hour workdays and not being able to join her friends at parties or sports events.

"Papa didn't know from baseball," she would tell my sisters and me when we balked at working in the store on weekends. And when the

Russ daughters did have the opportunity to socialize with friends, they usually declined. They were too tired, had to wake up too early for work the next day, and recognized that they smelled a bit too fishy.

A formal lunch break for the Russ employees would have been unheard-of. Lunch was usually a piece of bread with some lox or herring that was consumed in quick bites between waiting on customers. Sometimes Anne would steal away to have a favorite lunch of bananas and sour cream at Shwebel's Dairy Restaurant on the next block. On one such occasion she returned to the store quite sick to her stomach. She asked if she could go home. Her brothers-in-law refused. They assumed she was faking it, since she never really wanted to work. And what was she doing eating bananas and sour cream for lunch at Shwebel's, anyway? Wasn't there enough to eat right here in the store? She had an upset stomach, they said, a touch of food poisoning, and it

Anne behind the counter, waiting on a customer. She was probably about sixteen at the time, so this would have been around 1937. Hattie is behind her, closer to the front of the store.

would pass. But her sisters realized that Anne was quite ill and sent her home. When Bella saw how sick she was, she rushed Anne to nearby Beth Israel Hospital. The diagnosis: acute appendicitis that required immediate surgery. But there was nothing to worry about; the surgeon was a Russ & Daughters customer. Once he'd opened her up, the surgeon determined that she actually had a bleeding ovary. But as long as he was in there, "so it shouldn't be a total loss," he took out the perfectly fine appendix. Some time later the surgeon was shopping in the store and whispered to Grandpa Russ, "Your daughter has female problems. I suggest you get her married as soon as possible." So much for doctor-patient confidentiality in those days.

Anne met my father, Herbert Federman, through his mother, Mamie, who was a regular customer. One day while Mamie was shopping in the store she announced, "I have a son; he's the sheik of Brooklyn. Which one of the Russ girls is not married?" Anne was intrigued. "I'd like to meet the sheik of Brooklyn," she said. Anne and Herb were married in 1940. The affair ("maybe twenty people, tops," according to my mom) was held—on a Tuesday, of course—at Garfein's Catering Hall on Avenue A. Ida bought Anne's wedding gown at S. Klein's department store, on Fourteenth Street and Union Square. She paid ten dollars for it, and it fit perfectly. The newlyweds moved into a studio apartment on East Third Street, and the rest, as they say, is history. My history, to be exact.

Herbert, who quickly became known as Herbie, immediately took to the family business. Word of his talents as a slicer and a schmoozer (that's Yiddish for "conversationalist," although it definitely loses something in the translation) spread to customers who had moved from the Lower East Side to the Upper East Side and Upper West Side, to New Jersey and Connecticut. When they came into the store, they wanted the legendary Herbie to wait on them. Mr. Spanell was one such wealthy uptown customer, a fellow who had "made it big in plastics." He loved to watch Herbie slice his lox. Spanell thought that Herbie should put his hands to better use and made Herbie an offer: he would pay for Herbie to go to college and then medical school with no strings attached. When Herbie told Anne about the offer, she didn't need any time to think it over. "What do you need that for?" she said. "Don't you realize he'll own you for the rest of your life?" When Her-

The "sheik of Brooklyn," my father, Herbert Federman

bie turned down Spanell, Spanell stopped shopping in the store. And so Herbie wasn't owned by Spanell for the rest of his life; instead, he was owned by his father-in-law for the rest of his life. But that was different; that was family.

Joel Russ didn't insist on arranging the marriages of his three daughters, the way it had been done in the Old Country and for him here in America, but he did retain what is called in business today the right of first refusal. He would size up each potential suitor (and there were many for the three pretty, hardworking girls whose father owned a *store*

The store sometime before the 1950 renovation was completed. Herb is behind the counter; Murray, two unidentified men, and Grandpa Russ are in front of it.

and not just a pushcart), his evaluation based solely on whether this potential son-in-law would make a good worker for Russ & Daughters. Was he strong enough to schlep barrels of herring? Smart enough to add up a column of numbers on a brown paper bag? Could he make change? Would he look good behind the counter? Did he speak English well? (As the years went by, knowing Yiddish was becoming less important for dealing with our customers.) Fine, you can marry him.

In 1952, with his sons-in-law working in the store full-time and his daughters now tending to his seven grandchildren and working only on weekends, Grandpa Russ retired. Which is to say he would henceforth work only four or five days a week, not six. He had bought the building on East Houston Street that housed the store from the estate of Mrs. Franck, a German lady who had told Joel Russ in no uncertain terms that she would never sell her building to him while she was alive. Once he owned the building, he supervised the renovation of the store, which included adding a refrigerated showcase for the fish, so daily deliveries of ice were no longer necessary; installing a big kitchen in the back, complete with stainless-steel fixtures and terra-cotta floor tile; and putting down a new linoleum floor in the front of the store, which eliminated the need for sawdust and made for much easier cleanup (except when herring brine sloshed over the barrels). He broke through to Baskin's Bakery, the store next door, so he could add a candy counter near the entrance. And he officially settled into his retirement by bringing his old red leather chair, cracked and stained with fish oil, from his little office in the back and positioning it next to the candy counter, where he would continue to give orders to his family by pointing with his gold-handled cane and calling out "*Nisht azoy!*" (Not like that!) whenever anyone did something that displeased him. Until his death in 1961, everyone in and out of the family knew that Joel Russ continued to preside over the house that herring built.

From the East Side to the Seaside

In 1949, when I was four years old, Grandpa Russ moved the entire Russ family—his wife, his three daughters, their husbands, and the seven grandchildren—to Far Rockaway, Queens. As young as I was, I brought with me memories of the Lower East Side as being a dark, scary place. The suburbs, by contrast, felt open, free, and safe. Far Rockaway was a good place to grow up in the 1950s. We walked to school with our friends and came home for lunch. We played punchball and stickball in the streets, never worrying about cars. When a car came by, the driver waited until the boy at bat finished his turn. Everyone in our neighborhood was Jewish—cultural Jews who went to synagogue on the High Holy Days, had their sons bar mitzvahed (bat mitzvahs for girls didn't exist yet), and wouldn't let pork into the house but ate it in Chinese restaurants. The Italians and Irish lived on "the other side of town." Blacks lived in the housing projects. We had traded an urban ghetto for a suburban one.

It didn't take me long, however, to realize that my family was different from the other families in our neighborhood. I soon discovered that no other house had a "herring closet" in the vestibule, in which clothes that smelled of smoked fish and herring were to be hung before entering the main part of the house. Our house had one, and so did those of my grandparents and my aunts and uncles.

But it wasn't just the herring closets that made us different from other families. Most of my friends' fathers were accountants, engineers, lawyers, or teachers. They didn't work on weekends, so their families got to do all sorts of cool stuff together: attend baseball games at Yankee Stadium, Ebbets Field, or the Polo Grounds; ride the bumper cars at Rockaways' Playland or the Steeplechase parachute jump at Coney Island; choose from column A or column B at a local Chinese restaurant or eat a lobster dinner with the world's best biscuits and sandiest steamers at Lundy's; swim in the ocean at Far Rockaway Beach or in a pool at one of the fancy beach clubs that lined the oceanfront; or take evening strolls on the boardwalk while noshing a slice of pizza, a hot dog, or a knish.

Once Grandpa Russ had his daughters' husbands firmly ensconced in the business, the women's responsibilities were to be fruitful and multiply, and stay home with the *kinder*. They no longer had to work in the store during the week, but they were definitely expected to "help out" ten hours a day on weekends and holidays. At such times, my

Grandpa Russ, Grandma Russ,
and the gold-handled cane

sisters, Tara (born in 1943) and Hope (born in 1949), and I were left in the care of Grandma Mamie, my father's mother. Grandma Mamie was not your typical warm, sweet, protective grandmother. She was built like a tank (she stood five-foot-one and weighed about three hundred pounds) and cursed like a tugboat captain. She chain-smoked Pall Malls and ate everything and anything. Huge amounts of smoked fish and herring were brought home from the store so Grandma Mamie would have "something to nosh on" while she stayed in our home to "watch the kids." There was never any food left over by the time Sunday evening came around. The meals she prepared for us were usually combinations of whatever happened to be in the refrigerator at the moment. Her theory of cooking: "It's all going in the same end and it's all coming out the same end." There was no challenging her cooking, and she insisted we finish everything on our plates. Her own favorite snack was garlic rubbed on thick slices of pumpernickel bread, which were then slathered with chicken fat. Grandma Mamie intimidated everyone. In the middle of a serious punchball game in front of our house, she thought nothing of embarrassing me by screaming that it was time for me to come in for a nap. She then screamed at the other kids to "go play on your own block," even though she knew we all lived

The Russ clan at my cousin Paul Gold's bar mitzvah in 1956. I'm at the extreme left.

on the same block. None of my friends came into my house on the weekends when Grandma Mamie was in charge.

If we ever did something together as a family, it was on a Tuesday, when the store was closed. But this didn't happen very often: when Tuesday came around, my father was usually too tired to do anything. He preferred to soak in a hot bathtub most of the day and then putter around his basement tool room—he called it his "sanctum sanctorum"—where he was never to be disturbed. On Monday nights he hosted a poker game for his friends while my mother played mahjongg or canasta with her friends in another room. They always put out a big spread of smoked fish and herring, dried fruits and nuts, chocolate coffee beans and rum cordials, halvah and rugelach, all of which delighted their friends, who took home doggie bags filled with what they couldn't finish during the evening. On most other nights, he fell asleep in front of the TV.

When I did spend time with my father, it usually ended badly. He taught me how to ride a bike by letting go of it at the top of a steep hill. He taught me how to swim by pushing me into the deep end of a pool. He could be wonderfully playful at one moment but then, without warning, begin screaming and become menacing. While all of the customers and our neighbors loved "Herbie," I grew up angry and jealous that he never showed the same charm and patience with his own family. But when I attempted to fill his shoes behind the counter, I learned what it meant to be completely spent after a day of arguing with suppliers, customers, and employees. Everything was a fight in those days.

Father and Son Go Fishing

The best days with my father were when he took me to work with him. We left the house at 5:00 a.m., the same time we would have left to go on a real fishing trip. He drove the big red truck with its hand-painted sign in an elegant, old-fashioned typeface that I always felt was somewhat incongruous, given that it adorned a truck that was used for transporting smoked fish and herring:

Russ & Daughters
Queens of Lake Sturgeon

The first stops were to several Brooklyn smokehouses, looking for the one place that would satisfy my father that morning with the quality and amount of fish being offered.

The sights, the smells, the tastes—in a smokehouse, everything assaults your senses at once. Cavernous rooms with soot- and smoke-blackened walls. Intense smells, some sweet, others acrid. All manner of fish, submerged in their briny baths in huge steel vats, hanging from their tails punctured by wooden hooks, splayed out on racks going into or coming out of smoke-filled oven rooms, and finally packed into boxes, hundreds and hundreds of them lining the walls, ready for jobbers to deliver to stores, or to be picked up by merchants like Russ & Daughters who insisted on seeing, smelling, and having a taste from each lot of fish before buying it. It's an experience that either leaves you nauseated and disgusted or imprints your sensory memory in such a way that experiencing those sights, smells, and tastes again half a century later feels like coming home after a long trip.

The actual fish tasting was quite a show and followed the same script each time. (Although the store was named Russ & Daughters, and the presence and hard work of the Russ daughters was a large element of its success, not one of them ever went to the smokehouses. In those days, that was considered a man's job.) After carefully turning a fish skin side up and digging a small hole through its center so as not to damage its look and ultimate sale, a small sample was extracted, tasted, and then spit out. (A fish is split in two before it's smoked, so there are two pieces, each with a skin side and a flesh side.) Then came the discussion of whether this particular batch of fish was good enough to be sold at Russ & Daughters. Actually, it was more of a verbal brawl than a serious business negotiation. Particular catchphrases were always used: "This fish is uglier than you." "If you knew anything about fish, you wouldn't have to sell it to make a living." Shouting and cursing were the accepted forms of communication, and there was no attempt to tone it down at all, even in the presence of a ten-year-old boy. Looking back now, I suspect that part of the show was for my benefit, with the underlying message being, "Look, kid, every day is a battle. We enjoy our battles; it's all we know. But you don't need to do this for a living. You'll get a good education and won't have to sell fish."

After concluding business at the Brooklyn smokehouses and loading the truck with fish, we crossed the Williamsburg Bridge. There was always a traffic cop stationed on the Manhattan side of the bridge who recognized our truck, gave my father a wave and a big smile, and said "Hi, Hoibie." If there was enough time before the light changed, he might add, "Teaching your kid the business?" Cops were important people in those days. At the time, I had no intention of growing up to be a fishmonger, nor, I'm equally sure, would my father have wanted me to "take over the business." The plan was for me to go to college and become a professional; that was the unstated but clearly understood trajectory for most Jewish boys growing up in the 1950s. Yet there was something about those visits to the smokehouses and the acknowledgment from the cop at the bridge that made me feel that we were doing something special.

Our last stop before arriving at the store was Ratner's Dairy Restaurant on Delancey Street, just off the bridge. Unlike the smokehouse or our store just a few blocks away, Ratner's had the sweet aroma of freshly baked challah, rugelach, mandelbrot, apple strudel, and *mun* (poppy seed) cake. We walked to the back of the restaurant, where my father joined his cronies. Every day, it was the same people at the same tables ordering the same things for breakfast: "Poached eggs on toast, with tomato and cucumber." "Two eggs over easy, not too much butter, and a toasted bialy." "Farina with a big spoonful of butter and a side order of pot cheese to throw in." "Scrambled eggs, runny. Don't forget to bring the ketchup." And when the plates of food arrived, they reached for the salt and pepper shakers before even tasting the food. They drank endless cups of coffee that had to be brought to the table piping hot and to which they added cold heavy cream or half-and-half. And each man carried a little pill case, from which he would extract the tiniest tablet and throw it into the cup of coffee. It was saccharin, a sugar substitute, their perfectly serious attempt at weight control.

The waiters at Ratner's were legendary for their accuracy in taking and delivering orders but also for a gruffness that bordered on insolence. They shuffled over with trays full of food, and then unsmilingly and unceremoniously dropped the right dish in front of the person who ordered it. The waiter who often took care of our tables was friendlier than the others and would participate in the morning's conversation about which horse to pick at Aqueduct or which stock to pick on the Big Board. My father and the others always paid attention to his advice. At 8:30 everyone got up from the table, put some money by their plates (each man always knew just how much to put down as his share of the bill), and then went off to nearby stores or offices to start the workday. My father and I got back into the big red truck and drove the few blocks from Delancey Street to our store on East Houston. He let me unload the lighter boxes of fish from the truck as he unlocked the gates. For the rest of the day, he gave me jobs—filling in the candy bins, putting lids on red-and-white waxed containers filled with herring—that made me feel useful and productive. Sometimes I made the rounds with him to local diners and restaurants that bought wholesale from Russ & Daughters. If he couldn't find a parking space, I had to wait in the truck so he wouldn't get a ticket. If he could find a space, I went with him into the restaurant's kitchen, where he and the owner would light up cigars. "This your boy, Herbie?" the man would ask, looking down at me.

"Yeah," my father would reply. "I'm teaching him the meaning of C.O.D. Where's the money you owe me?"

Learning What It Means to Make a Buck

Once my sisters, my cousins, and I turned thirteen, it was time for us to "learn what it means to make a buck." Which is to say, learn firsthand how our parents made a living and why they came home every night smelling fishy. We were required to work in the store on weekends, either on Saturdays or on Sundays. There was no use complaining.

Cousin Nina once tried. She said she wasn't going and locked herself in the bathroom. Uncle Murray broke down the door. Cousin Paul was an athlete, the only one in the family. He got a dispensation if there was a game he had to play in on the weekend. I was jealous of Paul, not because he was an athlete but because he got out of work.

We were allowed to work only behind the candy counter, never behind the fish counter, where there were sharp knives. The first thing we learned was how to measure out candy for a customer. We scooped candy, dried fruit, or nuts into a large stainless-steel basin that was on the right side of an old balance scale. On the left side we put the appropriate disk-shaped weight or weights—they came in one-, two-, and five-pound increments. In the middle of this scale (which today sits prominently as a display piece in the store, having been replaced by a modern marvel with a digital readout) was a glass-enclosed viewer that had a movable arrow and several hatch marks, the largest and darkest in the center of the viewer. When the arrow and the center marker were aligned, the weight was correct. To get that alignment on one's first attempt at filling the basin with the proper amount of candy seemed to us kids like hitting a home run, except that no customer was satisfied

My cousin Nina Gold in front of the store, trying to look happy

unless the arrow leaned at least a tad past the center mark toward the candy basin, which meant that they got "good weight."

We learned how to ring the register and make change, now a lost skill, since digital registers determine and display the amount of change to be given. Today, it's almost impossible to hire someone who can both slice lox and make change.

Some things had changed since Grandpa Russ's era. The pay was good, $1.10 per hour, $11.00 per day, which was a lot of money back then. It was enough to buy bubble gum, Milky Ways, Three Musketeers, and other candies our store didn't sell; go to a double feature at the movies on a non-working Saturday; buy a slice of pizza and a Coke, and have money left over to buy baseball cards, comic books, and thousands of stamps offered "on approval" in the backs of those comic books. Our friends thought that we were rich. The work wasn't difficult, and we got to watch our parents in action as they greeted each customer as if he or she were a lifelong friend and then showed off each piece of fish as if it were a piece of fine jewelry. The only occupational hazard was those customers who felt it necessary to grab me by the cheeks and say "*Vhat a boychik!* Herbie, is he going to take over the store someday?" Of course, our parents had quite the opposite in mind.

Leaving Home

What they had in mind was education, and in the 1960s we all headed off to college. That's why they had worked so hard for all those years. Of course, the sixties were also a time of great social upheaval. Tara and Hope finished college and then both joined an ashram upstate. They were looking for answers. My parents couldn't even comprehend the questions. It had to do with "spiritual peace," my sisters said. Somehow, living in a commune, practicing yoga, and learning Sanskrit would make the world a better place. You can imagine the parental heartbreak and *tsuris* that their decision caused.

I went off to Alfred University, a small college in upstate New York, reachable only by a ten-hour trip on the Erie Lackawanna Railway and outside of the "call zone." (As in "Mark, it's Dad. I'm calling because I need you to come home and work in the store this weekend.") I was in a safe place, where I could be a big fish in a little pond and not have to sell it.

Though I had never before slept outside of my own house, never went to summer camp, there were enough Jewish kids at Alfred to make it feel knowable and comfortable. Some of my classmates came from the New York suburbs and were raised on weekend brunches of "appetizing." They asked to be notified whenever I got a care package from home, but my parents never sent smoked fish. (There were no FedEx overnight deliveries in those days, so shipping smoked fish was not a particularly good idea.) My care packages often included a salami from Katz's Deli, which was down the street from Russ & Daughters, and an assortment of hard candies from our store. I became the campus candy dispenser. "Hey, Mark, have you got a mint in your pocket?" This turned out to be very useful on Alfred's "dry" campus, with alcohol consumption officially forbidden. Although I came home for summer vacations, business was slow during those times ("dead" was actually the word my parents used), so there was no need for me to work in the store. But I always had some summer job that kept me financed for my new vices: cigarettes and girls. My father usually arranged these jobs by putting the arm on one of our customers. One summer I worked for an accounting firm and was assigned to audit the books of Ebinger's, a well-known Brooklyn bakery, at their main factory on Flatbush Avenue. It was a summer of significant weight gain. The following summer I worked for the New York City Parks Department, picking up garbage along the Rockaway beaches. An unexpected benefit from that job was that from the hard work and the nauseating smells, I lost the weight I'd gained the previous year working at Ebinger's. I spent another summer as a messboy and deckhand aboard oil tankers. It was there that I learned that the hard work in the store wasn't really as hard as I'd thought it was.

As a land-grant school (a school built on land given by the federal government to the state for the express purpose of building a college), Alfred University could and did require ROTC training for all boys during their first two years. After that, ROTC was voluntary, and most of the guys were glad to be done with the drills, the short haircut, and the spit-shined shoes. To this day I can't answer the question "Why did you volunteer to stay in?" When I began ROTC in 1962, the world (aside from the perpetual fear of an atomic bomb being dropped on us by the USSR) was a relatively quiet place. But by the time I graduated from college in 1966, Vietnam was on the map. I graduated with a bachelor's degree in liberal arts, a commission in the United States Army as a second lieutenant, and a deferment to go to law school.

I had been accepted by both New York University and Georgetown, so the choice was mine. My father offered me a free apartment above the store, which was within walking distance of NYU, but since there's no such thing as free anything, I knew that working in the store on weekends and holidays was part of the deal. So I chose Georgetown. My parents were okay with my decision. My education and career trajectory gave them the bragging rights they had long dreamed of. "My son, the lawyer" became an important staple of my father's conversation, whether he was chatting with a customer, a deliveryman, or a supplier, and no matter what the original topic of their discourse. Three years later I received my J.D. degree, and a few weeks after that I received a letter from the U.S. Army reminding me of my obligation and ordering me to report for duty.

I had a two-year commitment, and the army's plan was for me to spend one year at Fort Polk, Louisiana—famous for large mosquitoes and even larger rednecks—and then one year in Vietnam. This was not exactly what I had in mind, so I cut a deal with the army: two years anyplace in the world where there was an army base—my choice—and then one year anyplace they chose to send me. So I extended my tour by one year and spent the first two years in San Francisco. It was not bad. I had my own apartment near Golden Gate Park and drove to the base each day in my uniform. I viewed this as an office job with a dress code. The army extracted its pound of flesh in the third year and sent me to Vietnam. My father still had bragging rights in the store: "My son, the army captain . . ." But I suspect he swallowed hard for the last part: ". . . is in Vietnam.

It was 1971, and I was assured by those in the know that I would be stationed in Saigon and work as an army lawyer. But the army is big on bait and switch. When I arrived, I was quickly given orders directing me to an "advisory team" in the southernmost part of the Mekong Delta. I was to replace another officer who had been blown up in his jeep by a Claymore mine (used primarily in ambushes). I was loaded, along with a few tons of mail, into the belly of a large supply plane; there was nothing else on board. After a few hours the plane landed on a single strip of corrugated metal. The mail and I deplaned in the middle of a rice paddy in the middle of a monsoon in what looked like the end of the world. This was no place for a nice Jewish boy like me. After a month, I was transferred to Saigon and worked as an army lawyer.

Like many other returning vets, when I received my discharge from the army, I threw away the uniform. There were no brass bands welcoming us home. We were led to believe that we should be ashamed of our service, so it took years before we would admit to it. In any case, I was ready to begin my new life. When I returned to New York, I met my future wife, Maria, a beautiful young woman from South America. She lived just a few blocks from me and was working as a research scientist for a big pharmaceutical firm. I fell in love with her, as did my parents, even though she wasn't Jewish. We agreed that our children would be raised as Jews. Everyone was happy.

I also began what I thought would be a long and satisfying legal career. My first job, with Legal Aid, lasted less than a year. I quit when I came home from work one day to find that my apartment had been burglarized by someone who fit the description of one of my clients. Then I reversed roles and became a prosecutor. I joined the brand-new Office of the Special Prosecutor, which was created to combat the corruption in New York City's criminal justice system that had been brought to light by undercover police officer Frank Serpico. My job was to investigate and prosecute corrupt cops, judges, and politicians. At the time, I didn't know that some of these targets were also customers of Russ & Daughters. Finally, I joined a fancy uptown law firm as a trial lawyer. With two kids—our son, Noah, was born in 1975 and our daughter, Niki, was born in 1977—and a mortgage, it was time to make a living.

But the truth was, I wasn't happy practicing law. I worked long hours preparing for trials or going to trials. I came home every night with a stack of files under my arm that I had to study for the next day. I wasn't spending enough time with Maria and our children. Even when we were on a family outing, I feigned interest in the trip to the zoo or the afternoon in the park, but my mind was always on preparing for the next day in court. Yet the work and the work environment just weren't very satisfying. In a private law firm, you may be outwardly friendly with the guy in the next office, but you know that you're both competing for the next partnership that opens up. Looking back, I realize that I was searching for a way out of my legal career.

I found my thoughts going back to Russ & Daughters, and to how special a place it was. I saw how this little shop back in the old neighborhood gave my parents and their customers a sense of community, which was certainly not what I felt in that uptown law firm, and I realized that this was something I was searching for, too.

Keeping It in the Family

In 1978 I decided that I would keep Russ & Daughters in the Russ family. If this was something of a disappointment to my parents, who had worked so hard to send me to college and law school, they didn't let on. They actually seemed relieved; they had no other exit plan. Since the retirement of their lifelong business partners, Aunt Hattie and Uncle Murray, in 1976, my parents were also getting tired, and my father was increasingly weakened by his long-standing heart condition. My plan was to help them run the store part-time and practice law part-time. What was I smoking? The first day I took up my place behind the counter was the last day I practiced law. Even though I had worked there as a kid, I had no idea what it meant to be responsible for every piece of fish, every customer, and every employee every minute of the day. Little did I know that my career as a litigator would not prepare me for the battles of retail: for the endless negotiations with the suppliers, the employees, and the customers. So I began earning my Ph.D. (professional herring degree). And that was the beginning of a new chapter in my life.

It was all a bit too much for me to handle by myself those first few years, particularly after my parents retired in 1978. So I was happy when, several years into child rearing, with the kids well into daily school and after-school activities, Maria (who had quit her job after our second child was born) began to come to the store to "help out." Helping out initially meant paying the bills, keeping the books, and adding the feminine touch to the displays that the store had been missing since the retirement of the last of the Russ daughters. Maria also spoke Spanish, so she became my translator for communications with the kitchen staff, most of whom spoke no English.

I came to depend on Maria's participation in the business. There was no one I could trust as much—with my joys, my frustrations, and the cash. We traveled to work together and traveled home together. We discussed business morning, noon, and night. That part she hated. At parties, people would often want to hear my stories about the store. Maria wasn't terribly thrilled with that, either. It wasn't just that she had heard them all before; it was that the store had become our total preoccupation. When we socialized, Maria wanted to hear about everyone else's world, not ours.

Our family trips and family functions were scheduled around the store, just as Grandpa Russ had done. Weekends and holiday periods, when most people were celebrating or vacationing or just spending time with their families, were the busiest times for us. In order to go on a family trip, we would have to take the kids out of school. The one upside to working weekends and taking one day off during the week was that on our day off, the places we wanted to go to—department stores, movies, restaurants—were less crowded than they would be on weekends. Maria recognized other advantages to working in a family business: she had the flexibility to come and go as she pleased and was able to run home or to school if there was a problem with one of the kids. And she didn't seem to mind—she actually enjoyed—the hard work that the business demanded. She was often more physically active around the store than I was, and she would chide me when I spent too much time schmoozing when there was "real work" to be done.

As Noah and Niki grew older, we felt that it was time for them to learn, in my parents' inimitable words, "what it means to make a buck." How *did* Mom and Dad pay for the swimming, tennis, ballet, and skiing lessons, and all of the equipment that went along with them? And where *did* the money come from that would pay their tuition at Williams and Amherst colleges in Massachusetts, at Mount Sinai School of Medicine in New York, and at L'Institut d'Études Politiques de Paris? Noah and Niki had been in and out of the store from the time they were babies. In the beginning, it had been only a place to play: to hide behind the herring barrels, to ride on top of the fifty-pound sacks of onions being wheeled in on a hand truck, to swipe pieces of candy when their parents weren't looking. As they got older, they would learn that the store was actually a serious place of business. They would slice herrings, pack orders, answer phones, deliver packages, and work alongside their parents late into the night when the holidays came and the work demanded it.

Somehow, these childhood experiences took root in Niki as they had in me, and ultimately they brought her back to the store as an adult. But not Noah. From the time he was four years old and was giving anatomically correct names to the bones of the chicken we had just eaten for dinner, Noah had always wanted to practice medicine, and he followed his dream. As far as I know, I am the only Jewish father who was disappointed that his kid became a doctor. I was thinking sturgeon, not surgeon.

After college, Niki moved to the West Coast and was hired as assistant to the director of the San Francisco Museum of Modern Art. We missed her dearly and were quite happy when, a year and a half later, she said she was coming back to New York. I was not so happy to hear that she was going to work for an NPO, which, I was told, meant "not-for-profit organization." "We are the Russ family," I told her. "We sell herrings FPO [for profit only]."

When she left that job to plan her next move, I made my move—an offer of an apartment above the store, just as my father had tried to do with me. It worked this time, and it kept her within the "call zone." As in, "Niki, can you come down and help me with the phones?" "Niki, can you cover the candy side today, because Olga is out sick?" "Niki, can you help us through the holidays?" She agreed to work for us "temporarily," a word that in the Russ family has come to mean thirty to forty years.

So I would introduce Niki to the customers by saying, "This is my daughter, Niki. She's not only pretty, she's real smart." That was all true. But Niki didn't want to be known as my daughter; she didn't want to be known as anyone's daughter at that time. She left the business to spend some years finding her own way in the world. And I was left with a broken heart and a broken dream of father and daughter working together behind the counter.

In 2002, shortly after Niki declared her intention to leave, I received a call from my sister Tara's son, my nephew Josh. "Uncle Mark, I heard that Niki is leaving and I'd like to come into the business," he said. This was not the first time Josh had asked to come in. The last time, I had dissuaded him. Josh was raised in an ashram. His mother had moved there in the late 1960s in search of a spiritual and communal lifestyle. Many who did this quickly tired of ashram life and left after a year or two, but Tara stayed and raised her three children there. When Josh grew up, he left the ashram, went to school, became a chemical engineer, and worked for a high-tech company in Portland, Oregon. He never had much contact with the store, other than occasional visits, during which he spent most of the time pocketing candies from behind the candy counter. What could he possibly know about this business—what we sold, how we sold it, and how hard it was? But this time I suddenly saw Josh as a potential heir apparent. "Okay, Josh," I said. "You can come in and we'll see how it goes. No promises." I expected a very short-lived relationship.

Josh immediately impressed me with his approach to the business. He could go from point A to point B in a straight line, a crucial trait when running a business, but one that I could never master. I firmly believed that everyone who works in a small store, especially the owner, should be able to wear many hats and perform many jobs. I spent many hours of the day detouring from point A to point C, completely forgetting that I had originally set out for point B. But Josh, a trained engineer now selling smoked fish, was able to compartmentalize tasks and actually get them done. Moreover, Josh was my nephew and not my child. There would be no broken hearts if this didn't work out. I would teach him how to buy and sell fish the Russ way: in the smokehouses and from behind the counter; ten hours a day, six days a week. And guess what? He learned, and it worked out.

In 2006 I got a call from Niki. She had finished her walkabout—her exploration of business school, law, psychology, sociology, and nursing—and the wandering Jew wanted to come home. "Dad, I'd like to come back into the business," she said. I would not make that decision. I could not have my heart broken again. She would have to get the okay from Josh and from Herman, the manager of Russ & Daughters. They were running the business now, and they would have to decide whether they wanted Niki as part of their team. And they did. Four years later, in December 2009, Maria and I formally sold Russ & Daughters to Josh and Niki. In the Russ family, every generation inherits the right to buy out the preceding generation. It is an old family tradition, a tradition I am happy to keep.

Lox, Eggs, and Onions

SERVES 4

- 2 tablespoons canola oil
- 1 large onion, cut into ¼-inch dice (about 2 cups)
- 8 large eggs
- ¼ cup whole milk or half-and-half
- Kosher salt
- Freshly ground black pepper
- 1 tablespoon unsalted butter
- 2 ounces lox (about 2½ slices), cut into strips (or use scraps and wings)
- 2 tablespoons minced fresh chives

Heat the oil in a large, heavy skillet (preferably nonstick) over medium-low heat. Add the onions and sauté, stirring occasionally, until they are golden brown, about 20 to 30 minutes. Meanwhile, whisk the eggs and milk or half-and-half in a medium bowl. Season with salt and pepper, but go easy on the salt, as lox is quite salty.

Reduce the heat to low. Add the butter to the skillet with the onions. When the butter has melted, pour in the eggs. Sprinkle the lox and chives evenly over the eggs. Cook, folding slowly and constantly with a rubber spatula or large wooden spoon, until the eggs are set but still slightly wet, about 5 to 7 minutes. Taste and adjust with more salt and pepper as necessary.

3

The Employees

The Extended Family

As much *tsuris* as hiring family members gave Grandpa Russ, his situation became even worse when he employed people who were "strangers" at J. Russ Cut Rate Appetizing.

Jewish Revenge

Harry Eisenberg was a *shomer Shabbos,* a religious man and Sabbath observer who wouldn't work on Saturdays. But he knew how to run an appetizing store. When Grandpa Russ hired Harry in the late 1920s, they made a deal: Joel would work on Saturdays and stay home on Sundays. Harry would do the reverse. But then Joel demanded that Harry travel in from his home in the Bronx on Saturday nights—after sundown, of course—to help in the store with the late-night rush from the Yiddish theater crowd. Harry wouldn't. Instead, he quit. But not only did he quit, he also opened his own store two doors away, at 177 East Houston Street. The sign read

H. EISENBERG
CUT RATE APPETIZERS

That's Jewish revenge. At first, Grandpa Russ worried that Harry would steal his trade secrets as well as his customers. But by this time, Joel's three pretty daughters worked in the store. Hardworking and capable, they could slice lox, make change, and charm and disarm the most difficult customers. When they began working full-time in the store, Harry countered by bringing in his son, Murray—a nice boy, but not as good-looking as my mother and my aunts. No competition. Harry ultimately folded his store and went to work for another appetizing shop in the neighborhood. And Grandpa, knowing a good thing when he saw it, renamed J. Russ Cut Rate Appetizing. It became Russ & Daughters.

Ivan: Bowery Bum or Russian Noble?

Grandpa Russ made one other hire from outside the family. Since he wouldn't allow his daughters to schlep the heavy herring barrels, he hired Ivan. Ivan was an elderly Russian. It was hard to tell just how old he really was because a hard life had left him beaten and bowed. He was a drunkard from the Bowery when the Bowery, just a few blocks from Russ & Daughters, was home to cheap saloons, boardinghouses, and the alcoholics who frequented them. Ivan managed to get off the street because my grandfather allowed him to sleep in the back of the store and paid him a meager wage in return for working in the kitchen, peeling onions, filleting herrings, and washing pots and pans. Each morning Ivan schlepped three two-hundred-pound barrels of herring from the back of the store to the front sidewalk, ready for passersby to buy their herrings from one of the Russ daughters. Ivan kept up a running argument most of the day with some invisible form of deity. He would look up at the ceiling, shake his fist, and say something in Russian gibberish that no one understood—not even my grandfather, who spoke Russian. It was clear to all that Ivan held God responsible for his unhappy life.

There was a curious thing about Ivan. When it was time for a meal, he carefully washed his hands, took off his cap, sat at a tiny table in the kitchen, and meticulously arranged a plate with herring, smoked fish, and bread and butter, all of which he ate with a knife and a fork, displaying impeccable table manners. It was rumored that Ivan, the Bowery bum and herring-barrel schlepper, actually came from Russian nobility. But we were never able to find out for certain; nobody was willing to ask him.

Real Jews, Slicing Real Lox, with Real Attitude

Business boomed at Russ & Daughters during World War II. Selling canned goods "off-ration," or under the table, turned out to be quite profitable. And when the boys came home from overseas, things continued on the upswing. There was plenty to celebrate—peace, prosperity, family events—and Jews liked to celebrate with smoked fish and herring. Besides the retail store, we also had a successful wholesale business that supplied lox, smoked salmon, pickled herring, schmaltz herring, and chopped herring to Manhattan restaurants and luncheonettes. Since the Russ daughters now worked only on weekends and holidays, more help was needed.

Many returning soldiers were able to join their family businesses. Others took advantage of the newly created GI Bill and earned college or professional degrees paid for by the government. But there were also those who had neither a family business to fall back on nor an interest in higher education. Working in an appetizing store, a butcher shop, or a bakery would give them a trade and provide them with a decent living. We hired a few such men at Russ & Daughters.

Harry Pulvers, half brother to Uncle Max and therefore not technically a "stranger," came back from the Pacific theater something of a hero. He had been a combat soldier in the jungles of the South Pacific, and the family had high hopes for him as an employee. Tragically, he lived through the war only to die of a brain tumor shortly after being hired as a counterman at Russ & Daughters.

Another one of our countermen, a fellow named Sidney, was a sergeant during the war but was always evasive about whether he had actually been in combat. He did treat the store as a war zone, though: the counter was the DMZ and the customers were the enemy. But Sidney brought army efficiency to Russ & Daughters. He could slice a pound of lox—though a bit too thickly—wrap an order, prepare salads, fill in the showcase, and wipe down the scales all at once. Sidney also loved to give orders and seemed to forget that he worked for the family, and that they didn't work for him. So a guy named Steinie was hired as a sort of assistant counterman, to give Sidney someone to boss around. When Steinie left, Louie was hired to serve that same function, but that didn't work out well, either.

Sidney could best be described as a *farbissener,* someone who is bitter and angry at the world and whose greatest pleasure is to make those around him just as miserable. If he waited on you, Sidney made it clear that he was doing you a favor. You were a mere interruption; he needed to get back to the important work of slicing, packing, filleting, and cleaning. There was no time for schmoozing. Customers put up with Sidney's attitude because they believed him to be one of the Russes, a son-in-law, they thought. And Sidney didn't disabuse them of that notion when there were no real Russes around.

When I took over the store in January 1978, I realized how difficult it would be for Sidney to accept that he wasn't going to be the boss but, rather, that he would now be working for a *pisher,* a kid whom he had watched grow up. (And what could a lawyer possibly know about fish?) Sidney had always been a part of my life, behind the counter and at every Russ family function: bris, bar mitzvah, wedding, and funeral. So when I came on board, I gave him a raise, shortened his working hours, increased his vacation time, and gave him the title of general manager. None of it worked. He told everyone—suppliers, customers, and employees—that I didn't know the first thing about fish. In part I believed him and believed that I needed him, and because I needed him I put up with his bad attitude. Who else could I turn to? All the other Russes who knew the business were either retired or dead. Finally, in 1986, after Sidney had spent almost forty years behind the counter at Russ & Daughters, I forced him to retire. It was a painful experience.

Part-timers were hired for the weekends. Hy, Hymie, Al, and Dave had once owned their own appetizing stores, but they were now retired and waiting for the final exodus: Florida or Beth David Cemetery. While they waited, they wanted to keep busy, make a few bucks, and get out of the house. Appetizing had been their life. They knew smoked fish, and they knew how to make a sale. But their knowledge came at a steep price. They weren't going to listen to me. They told me when they would work, how much they would get paid, and how to run the business. And they couldn't get along with one another, either. At times they even faced off behind the counter with lox knives in their hands. I will say, it did keep the customers engaged while they were waiting for their orders.

The Postwar, Post-Jewish Labor Pool

The end of World War II hastened the exodus of Jews from the Lower East Side. Jewish veterans returned with a desire to participate in the American dream, which meant leaving the ghetto for the suburbs. In the 1950s Latinos—first Puerto Ricans, then Dominicans—began filling up the tenements that the Jews had once occupied and taking over the garment-center sweatshop jobs.

José Reyes and Herman Vargas, young Dominicans and cousins, were part of the new wave of immigration to the Lower East Side and therefore part of the new labor force as well. Their first jobs at Russ & Daughters were in the kitchen, peeling onions, pickling herrings, and washing dishes—clearly not what they had come to America for. But they did their jobs exceptionally well and with a positive attitude and spirit. About two years after I took over the business, I had finally had it with the motley crew of lox-slicing prima donna countermen that I had inherited. One day, in a fit of pique, I brought José and Herman out from the kitchen and put them behind the counter. Whatever the motivation, it was a bold move: placing Latinos behind the smoked-fish counter in a traditional Jewish appetizing store had never been done before. This was cutting-edge.

Our customers, the toughest New York has to offer, were not going to make this easy. It was understood that this was a Jewish store, selling Jewish food, prepared and sliced by Jewish employees. That was the culture, a given. Some customers were merely put off, some were offended, and some actually walked out. Their loss. As it turned out, these two men had talents I wasn't aware of. And as a result, both are still behind the counter and remain integral to the success and atmosphere of Russ & Daughters.

José has hands of gold and slices salmon with the skill of a great

José ("Yussel") Reyes

surgeon. He says very little but doesn't need to. Most customers are more than pleased just to stand there and watch this virtuoso at work. Slicing salmon for José is like meditation, and he is recognized by all as the Zen counterman. He is also our chief caviar packer; never is a single egg broken. ("I have José's hands insured by Lloyd's of London," I've been known to quip.) His place behind the counter is in the middle of the store. No other counterman would think of encroaching on his space or using his knife. José has been late only once in his thirty-five years at Russ & Daughters, and that was the day of the citywide blackout in 1977. He has also never been sick. He went to the doctor only once, when he got his finger caught and bruised in the showcase door. He comes to work perfectly groomed and leaves the same way even after ten hours or more on his feet behind the counter. For most of the years he has been with us, José wore several—eight to ten—heavy gold chains around his neck. Perhaps this was his way of saying to the world that he had "made it in America." But now he wears only a single chain with a single charm, the two-letter Hebrew word *chai,* which means "life." No doubt he is now secure in his place in the store and in the world. José is devoted to his customers, and they are just as devoted to him.

Herman has been featured in the Calvin Trillin novel *Tepper Isn't Going Out* as "Herman, the Artistic Slicer." And he is. But Herman also has the personality and charm of a great salesman, and a degree of patience and humility not normally found in the genome of Jewish appetizing-store workers. And to top it off, Herman also has an uncanny ear for languages. To the old-time customer who would attack him with "What do you know about slicing lox?" Herman would reply: "*Az ich ken lernen Yiddish, ich ken shneiden lox*" (If I learned how to speak Yiddish, I can slice lox). It was not long before those customers who used to demand a Jewish counterman lined up to wait for Herman to fillet their herring and slice their lox while he conducted a running commentary in Yiddish. And it was not long before the customers would ask me, "Where's the Puerto Rican kid who takes care of me, the one who speaks Yiddish?" (In those days every Latino in New York was identified by "native" New Yorkers—themselves either immigrants or children of immigrants—as a Puerto Rican, no matter where he came from.)

Herman ("Chaim") Vargas

Herman's natural abilities flourished in Russ & Daughters, and with the departure of Sidney I made him manager of the store. This was a lot of weight on his shoulders. Since his personality was nonconfrontational, he adopted the Tom Sawyer theory of management: paint the fence (in this case, fillet the herring) yourself, do it with a smile, and the others will naturally join in happily. Unfortunately, the other employees were happier just watching Herman fillet the herring, and I was not happy that I was still in the role of taskmaster. I repeatedly pressured Herman to "act like a real manager; tell the staff what to do, for God's sake." In response Herman found God, but not a new management style. I was never able to determine exactly what sect he had joined, but his new religion observed Saturday, not Sunday, as the Sabbath. He told me he was "required by God, the big boss" to take off on Saturdays. So there I was, a Jewish store owner, working behind the counter on Saturdays so that my gentile manager could observe the Sabbath.

Herman's newfound faith created additional problems. If a crisis arose that required immediate attention, analysis, and decision making, Herman's response was "Let's pray on it." He truly believed that through prayer God would provide an answer. So while he was praying, I was desperately trying to find a rational solution to the problem at hand. Each year as the Jewish holidays approached I would go into a frenzy about finding enough help to get us through a volume of business that was ten times larger than normal. We didn't need to have such a large crew on hand all year long, so these holidays represented a unique temporary-labor challenge. Herman would smile and assure me that "God will provide." I, less trusting in divine intervention than Herman, would place ads in the daily newspapers and impress into duty any relative within reach. Amazingly, each year one or more appropriate candidates would walk through the door. The interview process was a simple one: I would put a lox knife into their hands to see if they could slice fish. If they could, I would hire them immediately and then wait until after the holidays to sort out whether they were psychotic or were worthy of an offer of full-time employment. I never asked whether they had come to us as a result of one of my classified ads or by way of a more heavenly inspiration. In either case, our staffing problem was always solved and Herman would always remind me of the power of prayer.

Over the next few years there were countless times when I threatened to fire Herman, or at least replace him as manager, because his refusal to supervise the staff left me with the chore of constantly telling everyone what they should be doing. Herman's response was always the same: "Don't worry, God will pay you back for this." I was never quite sure whether this was meant as a blessing or a curse, so I didn't fire him. As it has turned out, Herman was and continues to be a blessing. His spirituality is a constant reminder of the beauty of what we do for a living, of the humility that is such an important part of serving the public. And he has always had my back.

In 2001 the Smithsonian Institution asked us if Russ & Daughters would participate in its annual Folklife Festival on the National Mall. Did I need this? Schlepping down to Washington, D.C., in the middle of the summer? Setting up a display of smoked fish under a tent? Talking to people who didn't have a clue about our products? But when Herman said he'd go with me, I knew everything would be fine. He'd be my sounding board. He'd calm me down. He'd be the go-to guy and get everything done. And he did. Herman set up a stunning display of fish. After giving my fish *shpiel* several times to clearly bored audiences, I told Herman I just couldn't do it again. He said he would give the talk; God would get him through it. And so my Dominican colleague Herman picked up the microphone and started talking about Jewish food. The audience—mostly from the Midwest—was completely absorbed and mesmerized. No one left.

Herman and José are now frequently referred to as Chaim and Yussel by our customers. Although they were born in the Dominican Republic with the surnames Vargas and Reyes, they have become Russes by virtue of their hard work, dedication, and passion. They both have the keys to the store.

The Russians Are Coming

The advent of computers—in many respects a boon to businesses—made hiring staff even more challenging. In the 1970s, '80s, and '90s, sitting in a cubicle in front of a computer seemed to many to be a better way of making a living than standing behind a counter. (And today, the reverse seems to be true. Go figure.) This further depleted the local labor pool. Pakistanis and Bangladeshis began moving to the Lower East Side, taking the place of Puerto Ricans and Dominicans who were moving up and out. Since these South Asians had no familiarity with our products, our customers, or our culture, hiring them wasn't an option.

In the late 1980s, HIAS (Hebrew Immigrant Aid Society) helped ease the way for an influx of Russian Jewish émigrés who arrived in the United States as the Soviet Union was beginning to collapse. Many came to New York City. I had hoped that this would be the answer to my recurring labor problems. After all, they were educated and they were Jewish—two key qualifications. And since they came from Russia, it was quite possible that they would even know something about our products. But I kept running up against one major stumbling block: none of these people had any idea of what it meant to work in a service industry—they barely knew how to smile, much less how to schmooze with the customers. Almost all of the Russians I interviewed said they were professionals, engineers mostly, and that smiling had never previously been a job requirement. I also realized that they had been raised and had worked within a Communist economic and political system, where there was no incentive to work hard or to be creative—two particularly important qualities for someone who is going to stand on his feet ten hours a day selling fish. I reluctantly gave up on the Russians.

Over the years, a series of characters have cycled through the store. The Jew for Jesus showed promise, but I had to let him go once he started proselytizing to the customers. I had high hopes for a trained chef who knew how to handle a knife and was professional in every way, except that he would disappear without notice for days, sometimes weeks. I never knew when he was coming back to work. Eventually, he just didn't. The defrocked South American priest was intelligent and good with the customers, but he had no idea how to make change. And when I put him in the kitchen in the back of the store to slice onions, he got insulted and quit.

Sometimes romance got in the way of commerce, despite my admonitions. I had hired a very young, beautiful, bright, and ambitious

Muslim woman from Uzbekistan, and I had great hopes of eventually putting her into a management position. A Muslim managing a Jewish appetizing store. Just think of the publicity possibilities. She lasted a few years behind the candy counter and then ran off with one of our Jewish customers. I was disappointed, but I have to admit that they are happy together—and they still shop in the store.

Sometimes an employee goes on to what the rest of the world would consider a bigger and better career: one former Russ & Daughters staff member is currently the director of an important New York State agency, another owns several major restaurants, and a third is a famous Hollywood producer. Occasionally I run into some of these former employees. Despite their successes, they often express a wistfulness for their days behind the candy or fish counter at Russ & Daughters—in my view, a simpler, less complicated, more satisfying work life.

The Newest Labor Pool

September 11, 2001, and the financial crash of 2008 brought a different level of job applicant to Russ & Daughters. Rarely in the past had I seen résumés at all; now there were curricula vitae piling up on my desk from professionals who had been downsized and wanted to seize the opportunity to change their lives. Post-9/11 was a time of introspection for many New Yorkers who realized they weren't happy as traders, lawyers, and bankers. They were looking for work that was more satisfying. What once seemed to be menial labor began to have greater appeal to many, as it became clear that baking bread, pickling vegetables, butchering meat, or slicing salmon has meaning in its own way and adds immeasurable value to our world. Elsewhere in this book I discuss what I consider to be the wondrous combination of art and science that goes into preparing the food we sell at Russ & Daughters. But there's more to it than that: as the counterman prepares that lox and cream cheese on a bagel for the customer who has ordered it, they talk. And more often than not, that communication has a magic of its own. As you are about to see.

Herring in Parchment

MAKES 2 TO 4 SERVINGS

- 2 pure salt herring fillets
- 2 to 3 cups cold milk
- 4 small new potatoes
- 2 tablespoons extra-virgin olive oil
- 1 small onion, halved through the core and thinly sliced into half-rounds
- 4 whole allspice berries, crushed
- 2 to 3 tablespoons unsalted butter, cut into thin slices

Put the herring fillets in a large, shallow bowl and cover with the milk. Allow the herring to soak for 2 hours. Meanwhile, bring a small pot of water to a boil. Add the potatoes and boil until they are tender when pierced with a fork, about 10 to 15 minutes. Drain the potatoes and set aside until cool enough to handle. Slice each potato crosswise into 8 rounds.

Preheat the oven to 400°F. Heat the olive oil in a medium frying pan or skillet. Add the onion and sauté until the half-rounds are golden brown, stirring frequently, 20 to 30 minutes. Stir in the crushed allspice berries.

Cut two circles of parchment paper, each about 12 to 16 inches in diameter. Fold each circle in half to make a crease. Arrange a layer of butter slices along the crease, down the middle of each circle. Top with a layer of potato slices, a layer of onion, and a herring fillet. Repeat with another layer of potato, onion, and butter.

Fold the parchment up over the fish to make a crescent shape. Crimp the edges tightly to make a seal. (If the parchment keeps unfolding, use a staple or two.) Carefully transfer the parchment packets to a baking sheet. Bake the packets until they are puffed, about 12 to 15 minutes. Serve the herring in the parchment. When you cut open the packets at the table, they will release a delicious, fragrant steam.

4

The Customers

I'll Have a Quarter Pound of Lox, One Filleted Herring, and Your Kishkes

Contrary to what most people assume, I didn't simply "inherit" Russ & Daughters. After years of working six days a week, ten hours a day, I earned the right to buy the business from the preceding generation of Russes. I did, however, inherit the customers. I'm retired now, but I can still hear them placing their orders from across the counter:

"I need a whitefish . . . It should be a nice one . . . My son, the doctor, is coming over for dinner . . . We want to introduce him to a nice girl . . . Her family is very well situated, thank you . . . Her father's a big shot . . . Maybe this will work out, please God, and I'll soon be a grandmother . . . No, don't give me that one from the top. What do I look like? A greenhorn? I want from underneath. No, not that one. The one next to it. No, that one's too dried out. You probably had that one left over from before the Flood . . . Why don't you go to the back and get me a fresh one?"

In these short exchanges there was always a life story: they had made it in America; their son was a doctor; it was time for him to get married and give them grandchildren; of course they would be involved in choosing his mate: she would be from a good family, a family at least as respectable as they were; the girl's father should be a "big shot." But make no mistake, although these customers might include me in discussions of family matters, they were still, first and foremost, seasoned shoppers. They had spent lifetimes struggling to succeed, and they were determined to make sure that no one took any of what they had achieved away from them. Now they would have only "the best." Don't try to pull any fast ones. Go in the back and bring out "a fresh one." There was always something to be learned from these old-timers. That was clear from day one.

"Private Stock"

January 2, 1978: It was technically my first day on the job after I had decided to go into the family business, even though I had been behind the counter since I was in utero. But I wasn't worried. How difficult could selling fish be? After all, I was better educated, more accomplished, and far more cultured than any of the employees or any of my relatives—both current and previous generations included.

That morning a giant limousine pulled up in front of the store, and out stepped a woman wearing a magnificent mink coat. She marched into the store and immediately demanded to see my mother, Anne.

"Anne always waits on me," she declared, "and she knows just what kind of sturgeon to give me and how to cut it."

"Well, I'm Anne's son, and I'm sure that I can help you," I said with my best counterman smile.

She said nothing else until I reached into the case where the sturgeon was displayed.

"Aaaaach!!" she screamed. It was the first shriek of disapproval from a wealthy middle-aged woman that I was to hear in the store; there would be many more in the years that followed. "No! Your mother gets me the private-stock sturgeon."

She pointed under the counter. She knew exactly what she wanted and where it was.

"Private stock" is a term that was the creation of and solely used by the Russ family to describe a particular type of sturgeon, the crème de la crème of all smoked fish, that has been culled from the regular stock because of its special fattiness, taste, and texture. Fatty fish have always been considered better because of their richer taste. As it turns out, they're better for you, too, due to their high amounts of omega-3 fatty acids, which reduce the body's cholesterol. Private-stock sturgeon was reserved for those customers who could appreciate the difference and were willing to pay the slightly higher price it commanded, sort of like a flawless diamond. But more than making a sale, what I wanted at that moment was to let this haughty lady know who I was: not a mere counterperson, not just the son of the owners, but a lawyer with a substantial curriculum vitae. Then I remembered that pleasing the customer was always the family mantra, so I kept silent and reached down below the counter to the hidden refrigerator where the private-stock sturgeon was kept. I brought it up to the cutting board with a bit of fanfare and proceeded to slice.

"Aaaaach!!" she screeched again, but this time it was not so much the sound of her voice that pierced through me as it was the look of total disdain that only a woman originally from the Lower East Side and recently made wealthy could muster up and deliver to someone who she believed was unfortunate enough to still be stuck in the old neighborhood and without an exit plan. Well, I was going to disabuse this woman of her arrogant assumptions—customer or not. As I looked up at her to deliver my response in my most lawyerly style, I disobeyed the counterman's first rule: never look away while you are slicing. Needless to say, the cut was deep and bloody. But before she realized what was happening, I excused myself and said that I would get someone else who would cut her sturgeon according to her wishes. She didn't seem disturbed by my sudden departure. In fact, she seemed relieved. With that, I went to the back of the store and sent a longtime counterman out to help her while I wrapped a towel around my bleeding hand, slipped out unnoticed, and went straight to the emergency room at Beth Israel Hospital, seventeen blocks north. More than thirty years later, the ensuing sixteen stitches and the scar from that cut are a reminder of the lesson I learned that first day from that tough customer. It's not important that I am a lawyer. When I'm behind the counter, I am a Russ who must remember what kind of fish each customer wants and how he or she wants it cut—and also remember never to look up while cutting it.

The Old-Timers

The old-timers invariably entered the store with attitude. Even before they crossed the threshold, they assumed that you were going to charge them too much, give them bad merchandise, or short-weight them. Bakers. Butchers. Fishmongers. All store owners were *gonifs* in their eyes.

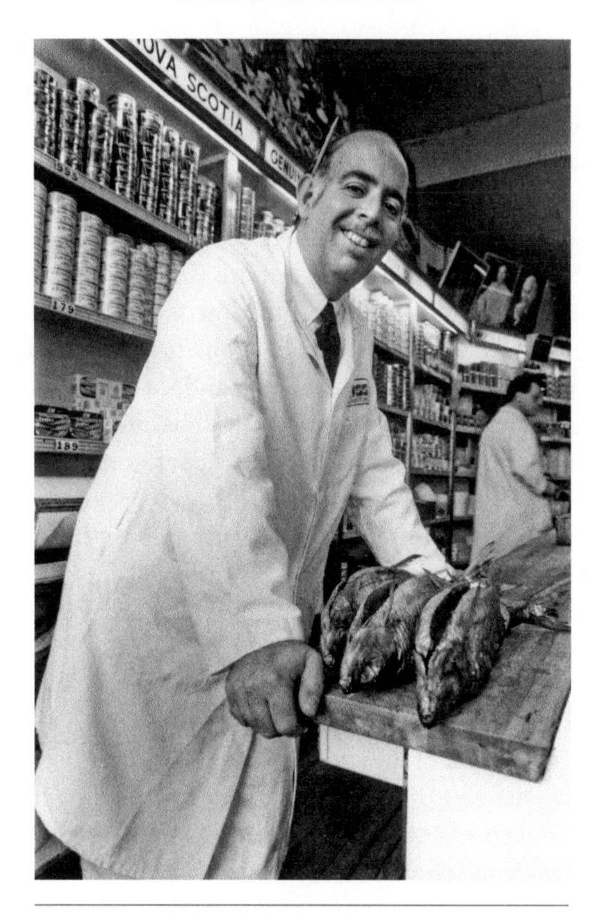

Me, behind the counter, in 1993.
Yes, I'm looking up, but I'm not holding a knife.
(Copyright © Harvey Wang)

Mrs. Schwartz entered Russ & Daughters, looking for canned sardines.

"How much for the sardines?"

"Three for twenty-five," said Grandpa Russ.

"Three for twenty-five? Ostrover around the corner has them three for twenty-one!"

"So? *Nu?* Go buy them by Ostrover."

"They're out of them."

"Lady, if I were out of them, I'd also sell them three for twenty-one."

. . .

How old do you have to be to be considered an old-timer? Sam, an immigrant from Russia by way of Czechoslovakia, became a successful zipper manufacturer in America. On his visits to Russ & Daughters, he would arrive via a chauffeur-driven car, perfectly groomed and in a suit and tie. He was obviously elderly, but he always entered the store straight of back and without any help.

One day, while I was schmoozing with Sam, he said, "I'm your oldest customer."

"Not even close," I responded, figuring that Sam was in his late eighties. We had customers well into their nineties.

Sam pulled out his wallet and proudly handed over his driver's license. Date of birth: 1905. This was 2008. Sam was 103 years old.

"Sam, you were born in Russia? Did you know about the Russian Revolution?"

"*Know* about it? I was *in* it!"

Sam was indeed our oldest customer.

One busy Sunday morning, I noticed an elegant-looking older gentleman with a full head of white hair standing quietly as he waited for his number to be called. He was dressed in a pin-striped shirt, a paisley tie, and a cardigan sweater; his gray pants were perfectly pleated. I'd never seen him in the store before, but after years in retail, I'd become pretty good at guessing age, ethnic background, occupation, and where people live. I figured this customer was an eighty-year-old WASP banker from the Upper East Side. To test that I hadn't lost my touch, I engaged him in conversation. It turned out that Ira was ninety-three years old and a recently retired kosher caterer from Brooklyn. I was impressed. In deference to his age, I asked him if I could get him a chair so he could sit while he waited his turn. He glared at me with obvious disdain.

"If I wanted to sit in a chair," Ira snapped, "I would have brought my own!"

No, he was definitely not a WASP banker from the Upper East Side.

. . .

And then there are the other customers, those who have shopped in the store for years and whose families have shopped with us for generations. They're not celebrities, but to us they are legendary because they have sustained us. They originally came in with their parents; now they bring their children and grandchildren, whom they will teach both how and where to shop for appetizing.

Mrs. Manny

"Mrs. Manny," as she referred to herself, had five children: four boys who had graduated from the best schools and were now very successful professionals, and a daughter. She and her late husband had raised these children on the Lower East Side. Now her grandchildren were attending Ivy League schools. She would *kvell* to us about all of them.

Every year, seven days before Rosh Hashanah (our busiest time of the year), Mrs. Manny would emerge from the subway on the corner of Houston Street and Second Avenue between 6:30 and 6:40 p.m., pushing her metal shopping cart. The store closed at 7:00 p.m. When she was spotted at the front door, the exhausted counter staff let out a collective groan. Some fled to the kitchen area in the back, while others went into slow motion with their current customers so they wouldn't have to wait on her. She was sweet but demanding. She demanded quality. She demanded value. She demanded service. Every year it fell upon me, the owner, to wait on Mrs. Manny.

Mrs. Manny came to Russ & Daughters every September to purchase eighteen herrings to take home and pickle. In Hebrew, the letters *chet* and *yud* combine to form the number eighteen, but they also combine to form the word *chai,* which means "life." Mrs. Manny gave each of her children three pickled herrings as gifts for the New Year and saved three herrings for herself to share with certain anointed neighbors.

For many years Mrs. Manny was content to buy her herrings from the display case in the front of the store. But that ended when she found out that Mimi Sheraton, then the restaurant critic for *The New*

York Times, was allowed to pick her herrings from the barrels in the back of the store. From then on, Mrs. Manny would accept nothing less when buying herrings for her family. Mrs. Manny and Mimi Sheraton were the only two Russ & Daughters customers ever allowed to go into the back of the store to select their herrings right from the barrel.

The actual process of choosing which 18 of the approximately 250 herrings in the barrel would go home with her was treated by Mrs. Manny with the same degree of gravitas as had been devoted, many years earlier, to deciding which of the many girls from the neighborhood she would allow her sons to "court," or which colleges they would attend. The battle, or rather the sale, would begin and end in the same way each year. If I was lucky, it would take a half hour. More often than not, it would take me way past closing time.

First I removed several layers of herring from the top of the barrel and put them into an empty bucket. It was understood that Mrs. Manny would never buy a herring from the top of the barrel. Then I reached into the barrel and fished out herrings one by one, holding each up and then turning it over and over in my hand for Mrs. Manny's inspection. It was as thorough an exam as any doctor would ever perform. While every barrel of herring that Russ & Daughters sold contained only top-quality herrings, Mrs. Manny was determined to find the "diamonds" in those barrels. And, I must say, she knew what to look for: clear, shiny, steel-blue skin, plump but firm flesh on the back, and no blemishes, marks, or bruises. Eventually, we found enough herring for her discerning eye.

Then she stopped showing up. There was no way of knowing what had happened. Did she get a bad herring that last year? Did she find a better place to buy herring? Did her doctor tell her not to expend her strength preparing herrings, or not to eat them anymore? Did she pass away? In some strange way, we missed her.

Some years later, my wife and I were having dinner with new friends, a couple from our neighborhood. At some point the husband and I began recounting stories from our Lower East Side roots. He was raised in a tenement above the shoe store owned by his father. There were five children altogether, all successful, and the four boys all went to Harvard Law School. He understood my daily life as a retailer because he and his siblings were required to work in their father's store on weekends and after school. The shoe store, named after his father, was Manny's.

He went on to tell us about his familiarity with Russ & Daughters. It seems that every year his mother would go to our store before the Jewish holidays to buy herring from the barrel, which she would then pickle, jar, and give to her children as gifts, as if they were the greatest treasures in the world. None of the children really liked pickled herring, but no one would dare tell her. But now that she had passed away, they miss both her and her pickled herring. I miss Mrs. Manny, too.

How to Impress Your Family

I hadn't seen Jeffrey for a while. The thirtysomething financier usually placed a big order once a year for breaking the Yom Kippur fast, but on this visit he reminded me that he had recently bought a big spread for Mother's Day "to share with my whole family," he said. "Even Grandpa Irving was there."

"How did it go?" I asked.

"It was unbelievable. I live at the U.N. Plaza, in a terrific apartment overlooking the East River. You can see three bridges from my windows. I was made a partner at the hedge fund where I control two billion dollars' worth of investments. I have a beautiful girlfriend, and she's *Jewish* [emphasis his]. But not once did Grandpa ever acknowledge any of my successes or accomplishments. Then, in the middle of this family get-together, he comes over to me with a plate full of smoked fish and says, 'Jeffrey, belly lox from Russ & Daughters? You must be doing very well.' "

Customers like Sam, Ira, Mrs. Manny, and Grandpa Irving started out on the Lower East Side, then moved to apartments uptown or homes in the outer boroughs or suburbs. They owned businesses with their names on the front door, and they raised children who went to the best schools and became professionals. Their success was the result of hard work, grit, intuition, and an intelligence that had nothing to do with book knowledge. These customers never allowed anyone to condescend to them; they remained in control of any situation. And they never accepted a helping hand—not a chair to sit on or a taxi ride home. They were once the typical Russ & Daughters customer; now they are few and far between. A dying breed. I miss them.

Herring Purveyors to the Stars

There are many stories about famous people who shopped at Russ & Daughters. Some are verifiable, others not quite truthful. I was told that Eleanor Roosevelt once came to the store, but upon close questioning of Aunt Hattie and my mother, the customer turned out to be a friend of the store's landlady who, in turn, "knew" Mrs. Roosevelt. But both Aunt Hattie and Mom assure me that Bernard ("Barney") Baruch's chauffeur was indeed in the store and did buy fish. (They naturally assumed that the fish was intended for Mr. Baruch's table and not the chauffeur's.) I can verify the story that the gangster Bugsy

Zero Mostel, showing his appreciation to Aunt Hattie
(Copyright © Mal Warshaw)

Siegel was a customer, because from time to time I still hear from his granddaughter, who requests that we ship her schmaltz herring to Las Vegas and asks that they be "just like the ones my grandfather got from your grandfather."

Many celebrity customers who were born on the Lower East Side and then moved away as fame and fortune allowed would come back to buy fish. Yiddish theater stars Molly Picon, Jenny Goldstein, and Aaron Lebedeff worked nearby and were regular customers. Zero Mostel frequently came in to buy belly lox and herring. According to family legend, Zero had wanted to marry my mother. One day he asked Grandpa Russ for her hand in perfect Yiddish. Grandpa Russ wouldn't have any of it. Zero was a *gantseh meshuggener* (a total nut) with his constant *tummeling* (commotion making). And, worst of all, he was a *batlan* (someone without a regular means of earning a living). As it turned out, Zero was already married. You could never tell when

Zero also liked to help out behind the counter
(Copyright © Mal Warshaw)

he was kidding or being serious. One time he went behind the counter, sliced a bagel, and starting buttering it in the palm of his hand. To the delight of the other customers, he continued buttering all the way up his shirtsleeve.

Alexander "Sasha" Schneider, a renowned violinist with the Budapest String Quartet, was known as a tough, gruff, and impatient customer who loved his schmaltz herring. Schneider was born in Vilna, Lithuania, in 1908. The Litvaks, as Jews from Lithuania were known, claimed to speak a better Yiddish and to know more about music, art, literature, and food than their fellow Jews from less rarefied parts of the Diaspora. This knowledge included herring, of course. Sasha would show up at the store with a large round loaf of peasant bread under his arm. (He so loved that bread that he invested in the SoHo bakery where it was baked in wood-fired ovens.) As soon as he walked through the door with his bread, the largest, fattiest schmaltz herring in the case was gutted, skinned, and sliced. Sasha was then accompanied to the kitchen in the back of the store, where a bottle of vodka was kept on ice just for him. He relished each slice of herring, eating it not with the delicacy and finesse of a virtuoso violinist but with the urgency of a Jew expecting an imminent pogrom. Each bite of herring was followed by a piece of bread roughly torn from the loaf, and then chased with a shot of vodka. After two or three rounds of this ritual, Sasha would begin telling stories about growing up in Vilna: in particular, how his father, a construction worker and amateur flautist, demanded that he and his siblings practice their instruments—cello, violin, or piano—four to five hours every day. He always finished his herring and his stories by saying, "Deese jung people today dun't know vhat it is to practice; and dey dun't know a goot herring."

The celebrities keep coming to shop at Russ & Daughters. Artists, musicians, writers, actors, politicians, chefs, and restaurateurs, they are too numerous to mention here, and besides, we respect their privacy. They come in quietly, not identifying themselves, dressed down and relaxed. Just like everyone else, they take a number and wait their turn, wanting only to buy their bagels and smoked fish and then go home to enjoy it all with family and friends. We are honored by their patronage—as we are by all of our customers'.

Niki, Josh, and Herman behind the counter.
Anthony Bourdain is in front.

Neither a Giver nor a Taker Be

Grandpa Russ believed that family members should never accept gifts from customers or socialize with them outside the store. He never wanted to feel obligated to give a customer a special piece of fish or a discount in exchange for a favor. There would be no *hondling* (haggling or bargaining) in his store. That was for the pushcarts on the street. The Russ girls had this drilled into them as soon as they started working in the store. But my father and my uncles weren't born Russes. They often ignored this unwritten rule.

My father loved to buy goods from customers who were wholesalers or manufacturers. We sold retail ourselves, and we considered ourselves way too smart to *buy* retail. This often led to problems. For instance, my father once gave my mother for her birthday not one but a wholesale lot of a dozen of the same sweater, in assorted colors. Too bad if she didn't like any of them, because they couldn't be returned and she couldn't say anything that might be perceived as negative to the customer who manufactured them. Dad also thought nothing of using customers as his lawyer, insurance agent, stockbroker—even his bookie. This often ended badly, with my father losing money and the store losing another customer.

There was one exception to the Russ family prohibition against granting favors to customers. Special attention was given to the "biggest" doctors. You never knew; they might be needed someday. Uncle Murray, for example, would think nothing of asking a famous ear, nose, and throat specialist to interrupt his shopping and take a look at his sore throat. Invariably he would be told to stop smoking. For that advice, Uncle Murray never gave a discount. But for those doctors who told him not to worry about the smoking, he would go in the back and find a special piece of sturgeon or whitefish.

Grandpa Russ wouldn't approve, but I have met some of my dearest friends across the counter, and it's never been a problem. There were times, however, when I paid too much attention to customers at the wrong moment, listening too carefully when I should have been just slicing. When I heard one customer telling another to buy stock in a fried chicken franchise, I invested in that stock. I watched as the stock went from pennies to dollars, and continued to watch as it went back to pennies and then disappeared. I did the same thing when I learned that a customer had started a biotech company that he claimed had developed a cure for cancer. I finally sold the stock at a substantial loss, after he went to jail. From then on, the only stock I bought was what I could sell in the store. My only long-term investment was in herring futures. Fortunately for all of us, I didn't know that Bernard Madoff was a customer until the publication of his credit card slips showed several purchases at Russ & Daughters.

Art for Fish

The Bowery, Lower East Side, and East Village neighborhoods that surround Russ & Daughters were for many years home to young artists looking for cheap housing. (The old Provident Savings and Loan Bank building on the corner of East Houston and Essex was Jasper Johns's studio in the 1970s.) Many of those starving artists would come into the store and offer to barter art for fish. I admit that I have no eye for and no interest in art, so I always passed. But on one occasion, I broke my rule and visited the Bowery loft of an artist customer. As he was showing me his canvases, I remarked that one painting with a large brown circle looked "just like a bagel." This was obviously not the response he had been expecting. He quickly showed me out and stopped coming to the store. I do like to read and listen to music, and I am quite proud of my collection of autographed books and CDs, which I happily accepted in exchange for sandwiches. Don't tell Grandpa Russ.

The Art of the Schmooze

You're either born a great schmoozer or you're not. Grandma Russ was always happy to schmooze. Since she spoke so little English, her schmoozing was limited to Yiddish with the pushcart vendors on Orchard Street. They were happy to schmooze with her because she was one of their few customers who never *hondled.* Grandpa Russ, on the other hand, had neither the time nor the patience to schmooze. But Aunt Hattie and Aunt Ida were great schmoozers; they could charm a herring right out of the barrel. My mom took after her father; no patience for schmoozing there. But my dad was a natural-born schmoozer, and the customers lined up to be waited on by him. I was lucky enough to inherit the family schmoozing gene. Maria is a terrible schmoozer. Whatever the opposite of a schmoozer is, that's Maria. Fortunately for our business, Niki is an even better schmoozer than I am. Josh is not a natural-born schmoozer. Until he came into the business he was an engineer, and they are not known for their schmoozing skills. But he has other essential qualities. For example, Josh finishes one task before starting another, a definite asset in running a business. Schmoozers, on the other hand, have difficulty getting things done; they're too busy schmoozing. But as I have watched Josh run the business these past few years, I have seen his ability to schmooze improve along with his slicing skills. Customers now line up to wait for Josh to slice their salmon and listen to their stories. Behind the counter, he has become his Grandpa Herbie, world-renowned salmon slicer and schmoozer.

People who are born schmoozers often go into retail businesses, usually small, family-owned ones. They like, and maybe even need, the personal interactions such places offer. People shop in small retail stores because they, too, like—and maybe need—that same personal interaction. Among people who work in retail, the great schmoozer doesn't just talk but also knows how to listen. The ability to be a good listener is derived from a basic love of people. This must be genuine. It cannot be faked. There is no doubt in my mind that this joy in listening to people, in hearing their stories, sharing in their *nachas* and their *tsuris,* is genetic in origin. The schmoozing gene will soon be mapped.

Some things distinguish a great schmoozer from a merely good one. The ability to make the customer feel as if he or she is the only thing the schmoozer is interested in at that given moment is essential. To achieve this, you yourself must feel that this customer is your friend, and that the interaction is personal as well as commercial. Of course, the schmoozer must not forget that he is running a business, so this is where multitasking comes in. While listening intently, eyes and ears fixed on the customer, the schmoozer will be able to notice that there are dirty spots on the showcase, herrings in disarray, salads that need to be filled in, and a ringing phone that needs to be answered. A truly great schmoozer can direct other people to accomplish these tasks without ever taking his focus away from the customer with whom he is schmoozing. A good memory is essential, even if you are a natural-born schmoozer. Memory for names is a given, not only the name of the customer as he or she walks in the door but the names of the customer's spouse and children, as well as any *tsuris* or *nachas* related during the last visit. A quality schmoozer remembers what the customer bought last time, which part of the fish he prefers, how she likes it sliced. The perfect schmooze must be a seamless resumption of your last conversation, even if the customer's last visit was six months ago. For example:

The good schmoozer: "Hello, Mrs. Schwartz. How's your daughter Rebecca?"

The great schmoozer: "Hello, Mrs. Schwartz. How's your daughter Rebecca? Did she recover from that twisted ankle? Did you help take care of her two kids, Betsy and Andy? Your grandchildren are so adorable. And smart, too."

The great schmoozer will attempt to bring other customers into the schmooze. When two or more customers are introduced into the schmooze, they are likely to discover things they have in common: their kids go to the same school, their grandparents came from the same shtetl in Poland, they used the same "top" doctor for hip-replacement surgery. This provides them with a more unique experience, a story to tell over the salmon and bagels when they get home. The schmoozer is humble, more of a good listener than a good talker. While the customers may ask the schmoozer personal questions, that is merely a rhetorical device. They don't really want to hear about you; they want to talk about themselves. And since they are spending their money in your store, your conversation should be about them. The schmoozer must be able to distinguish between *nachas* and *tsuris,* and show the appropriate amount of joy or sympathy, depending on the individual situation. This is not always as easy as it seems. Of course, a birth, bris, bar/bat mitzvah, or wedding is clearly a major *nachasdik* life event that requires a great display of empathetic joy. Illness, death, and investments with Bernie Madoff clearly fit into the *tsuris* category. But be careful: divorce, which could be *tsuris* for the son who is being divorced, might be regarded as a joyful occasion by the mother who never liked her daughter-in-law in the first place.

I learned something very interesting during my years of schmoozing with my customers: the less you say, the greater the aura of knowledge and wisdom you acquire. From years of schmoozing, I came to be regarded by some of my customers as a *chochom,* a wise man, and I was often asked for my opinions about politics, finance, international relations, religion, and even car repair. Of course, true schmoozer and *chochom* that I am, I would never give them.

Truthfully, beyond the fish we sell, I know very little about anything else. It is assumed that I am a repository of great bits of worldly knowledge just because for thirty years I stood behind the counter in the same store in the same neighborhood and sold the same fish products that my family had been selling for a hundred years. So I try to accept the role with some grace, and have grown a beard—by now a very white beard. I continue to say very little and listen very well, and at least try to look the part.

From Oy to Yo

When I started working in the store in 1978, most of our customers were Jewish and over sixty. Very few of them still lived in the neighborhood. Today, maybe 50 percent of our customers are Jewish, and most of them are in their twenties, thirties, and forties. Being the schmoozer that I am, I ask them where they live. Many reside in the now-hip neighborhood of the Lower East Side, on Rivington, Essex, Stanton, Ludlow, Orchard, or Delancey Street, in buildings that earlier generations couldn't wait to move away from (and that have, I should add, been breathtakingly refurbished). "What do you do for a living?" I ask. Design clothes and websites, make movies, write, blog, et cetera. If they're carrying a guidebook, I ask them where they're from. If someone speaks with an accent nowadays, it's a French, Italian, German, Spanish, Australian, or British one—rarely Yiddish. Some customers who live outside the neighborhood still come by subway, some by car, and some by limousine. But we recently installed a bike rack outside the store for those who like to burn calories before eating their bagels and lox.

Though the customers and their ethnic origins, accents, and professions have changed through the years, they continue to come to Russ & Daughters for something more than a slice of smoked salmon. They come for the one-of-a-kind experience. And the schmooze.

Beet, Apple, and Herring Salad

MAKES 6 TO 8 SERVINGS

BEETS

6 to 8 medium beets, trimmed and scrubbed (about 1¾ to 2 pounds)
¾ cup red wine vinegar
3 tablespoons vegetable oil
3 tablespoons sugar
2 teaspoons mild Swedish mustard

MUSTARD SAUCE

3 tablespoons red wine vinegar
2 tablespoons mild Swedish mustard
1 tablespoon sugar
1 tablespoon honey
¼ cup vegetable oil
1 tablespoon minced fresh dill
Kosher salt
Freshly ground black pepper

SALAD

1 medium Granny Smith apple, peeled, cored, and cut into ¼-inch dice
1 small red onion, cut into ¼-inch dice
2 pickled herring fillets, cut into ¼-inch dice
¼ cup minced sour pickle

To prepare the beets, place them in a large saucepan and add water to cover. Bring to a boil, reduce the heat, and simmer until the beets are tender, 30 to 45 minutes. Drain the beets and rinse with cold water until they are cool enough to handle. The skins should slip off easily. Cut the beets into quarters.

Whisk the red wine vinegar, vegetable oil, sugar, and mustard in a large bowl. Add the beets and toss to coat. Allow the beets to stand in the vinegar mixture for 2 hours.

Meanwhile, prepare the mustard sauce. Combine the red wine vinegar, mustard, sugar, and honey in a medium bowl and whisk to blend. Slowly pour in the vegetable oil, whisking constantly. Whisk in the dill and salt and pepper to taste.

Drain the beets and cut them into a ¼-inch dice. Place them in a large bowl and add the apple, red onion, herring, and minced sour pickle. Pour half the mustard sauce over the salad and toss to blend. Add more mustard sauce a little at a time until the salad is well coated. Taste and adjust the seasoning with more salt and pepper as necessary.

Fruit Strudel

YIELDS 2 STRUDELS, ABOUT 8 TO 12 SLICES EACH

- 1½ cups dried apples
- 1 cup dried Turkish apricots
- ½ cup pitted prunes
- ½ cup golden raisins
- 1½ cups boiling water
- ½ cup chopped toasted walnuts
- ¼ cup packed dark brown sugar
- 1 teaspoons cinnamon
- 10 sheets phyllo dough, thawed
- ¼ pound (1 stick) unsalted butter, melted
- 1 cup breadcrumbs
- 1 large egg yolk

Put the apples in the work bowl of a food processor and pulse until coarsely chopped. Transfer the apples to a medium pot. Repeat with the apricots and prunes. Add the raisins to the pot. Pour in the boiling water, stir, and cover the pot. Allow it to stand overnight.

Arrange racks in the upper and lower thirds of the oven and preheat it to 350°F. Line two baking sheets with parchment paper.

Stir the walnuts, brown sugar, and cinnamon into the dried-fruit mixture. Place one sheet of phyllo dough on one of the baking sheets. Brush lightly with the melted butter and sprinkle lightly with the breadcrumbs. Repeat four more times, stacking five sheets of phyllo in total. Spread half of the fruit mixture lengthwise down one edge of the phyllo, leaving a two-inch border at either end. Fold in the ends over the fruit and roll up jelly roll–style to form a log. Arrange the log seam side down in the middle of the baking sheet. Make another log on the other baking sheet with the remaining phyllo, butter, breadcrumbs, and fruit filling.

In a small bowl, whisk the egg yolk with 2 tablespoons of water. Brush the egg yolk mixture over the logs. Bake the logs until they are puffed and golden-brown, about 30 minutes, rotating the baking sheets from top to bottom halfway through the baking time. Cool the logs on the baking sheets, then cut crosswise into thick slices and serve.

5

The Neighborhood

From Pushcart to Posh

Sometime in the 1980s, Ruth Abram, a lovely young woman from a prominent southern Jewish family, invited me to lunch. Believing that I was a person of some weight in the neighborhood, she wanted my opinion regarding her idea to convert a Lower East Side tenement into a "museum of immigrant life." Great. Another out-of-towner with romantic notions about the Lower East Side. What could she possibly know about what life was like in these tenements and on these streets? Didn't she understand that from the beginning this was a place people were desperate to leave?

I gave her my usual diplomatic opinion: "What? Are you crazy? Who's going to visit your museum? A few nostalgic New Yorkers? Maybe a few Jews from New Jersey? But no one from Iowa or even Connecticut is coming to this neighborhood. You need to understand the Lower East Side before you invest your time and money in this *farshlugginer* [valueless] scheme. After the ribbon cutting, you'll be selling admissions and nostalgia. I sell fish and nostalgia, and even that's not so easy to do on the Lower East Side these days. At least they can eat the fish."

Fortunately, Ruth didn't take my advice. The Lower East Side Tenement Museum at 97 Orchard Street opened in 1993 in an 1863 tenement building that, over the years, was home to seven thousand immigrants from twenty countries. They now welcome almost two hundred thousand visitors a year.

Pushcart Nation

As far back as the 1870s, the Lower East Side of Manhattan was a ghetto of shoddily built tenements designed to maximize financial return to builder, landowner, and tenement owner. As many people as possible—

for the most part, newly arrived immigrants—were stuffed into tiny, airless apartments in four- and five-story buildings, with tenants often renting out a small space within an apartment to even newer greenhorns.

The typical early tenement apartment was about 250 to 300 square feet and contained a coal-fired stove and a bathtub in the kitchen. A single bathroom in the hallway was shared by the residents of every apartment on the floor. During sweltering city summers, families slept on fire escapes to get some relief from the heat. Disease and urban epidemics took a large toll on these residents, who lived in unsanitary, crowded conditions. Grandpa and Grandma Russ lost their firstborn, an eighteen-month-old boy, to the 1910 typhoid epidemic that swept through New York.

Employment options for the new immigrants were limited. Men, women, and even children would stand on street corners, hoping to be chosen for some menial day labor. If the newcomer was lucky, he or she might be chosen for piecework, assembling men's or women's clothing in one of the local tenement apartments that doubled as satellite garment factories. These sweatshops were notorious for their lack of light, air, and sanitary facilities, and for the low wages the workers were paid. The workers' living accommodations were not much better. For two or three dollars a week, they could board with a tenement-dwelling family who would rent out any beds that were not already occupied by family members; this would help them to make their own rent payments.

The media of the day, much like today's media, often sensationalized life on the Lower East Side, highlighting the criminal gangs, gambling dens, and brothels in the neighborhood. Slowly, the appalling conditions began to attract the attention of progressive reformers such as the photojournalist Jacob Riis and the public health advocate Lillian Wald. And gradually things began to change for the better: laws were passed that regulated the amount of ventilation a tenement apartment had to contain, sanitary conditions improved, and social welfare agencies taught the immigrant families how to improve their lives and their living conditions. Ever the rugged individualist, Grandpa Russ had no patience for the "do-gooders" and their social welfare agencies, which included such legendary facilities as the Educational Alliance, the Henry Street Settlement, and the Hamilton-Madison House. He wanted success in America, but to him and most other immigrants, moving up meant moving out of the Lower East Side.

By the 1920s, bridges, subways, and elevated train lines linked Lower Manhattan to the outer boroughs. As a result, people moved as quickly as they could afford to from the Lower East Side to Brooklyn, Queens, and the Bronx. The Immigration Act of 1924 imposed strict quotas on the number of immigrants, particularly Eastern Europeans (i.e., Jews) and Southern Europeans (i.e., Italians) who could enter the United States. But the tenements remained full, and there was no incentive to upgrade or even to make repairs to them. Instead, there was a movement to "restructure" the Lower East Side. Grandpa Russ joined the East Side Chamber of Commerce, an association of developers, landlords, bankers, and small merchants who shared a vision of the Lower East Side as a middle- and upper-middle-income "walk to work" residential community servicing the expanding financial industry of Lower Manhattan. It was perfectly situated between uptown and downtown. Restructuring meant slum clearance and relocating the street vendors into brick-and-mortar markets. The plan was to construct high-rise apartment buildings, complete with green spaces, along an East River promenade to attract the growing middle class to the neighborhood. But the stock market crash of 1929, the ensuing Great Depression, and World War II put most of these plans and dreams on hold for the next sixty years.

A few of the plans did come to fruition. The Second Avenue Elevated Line, which started above Allen Street and made the streets underneath it a dark haven for crime, was finally torn down. Prostitution had been a thriving business under the El, and many of the prostitutes had names like Goldstein, Ginsberg, and Schwartz. Allen Street was widened and turned into a tree-lined mall; it was to be a "speedway" for cars going uptown. Aunt Hattie remembers that in 1928 Mayor Jimmy Walker attended the unveiling of the new Allen Street. She also remembers that a few years later he resigned and fled to Europe to avoid prosecution for corruption.

As if the Depression wasn't bad enough for business, in the 1930s the city began digging up Houston Street for the IND subway line, which was to include a stop on the F train right across the street from Joel Russ's little appetizing store. Buildings were torn down to widen the street, and a huge hole was extended almost to the curbline. The few customers who were able to put together a couple of cents found it almost impossible to cross the street to spend it on a herring.

The consortium of landlords, developers, and small merchants (some, including Grandpa Russ, who had been pushcart peddlers themselves) focused their attention on getting rid of the pushcarts. To them, this way of doing business was old-fashioned, unsanitary, and inefficient, and they had an ally in Mayor Fiorello La Guardia. By 1940 their efforts had paid off, and most of the pushcarts had been relocated to newly constructed indoor stalls in the Essex Street Market and the First Avenue Market. They were a great success, and to everyone's surprise (the peddlers' as well as the consortium's), customers who had moved away from the neighborhood continued to come back to shop at their favorite pushcart stands—even if they were now indoors. The idea of a clean but atmospheric indoor market also proved to be an attraction for the "uptowners" and for tourists looking for some Lower East Side flavor and nostalgia. But truth be told, without the pushcarts on the street, some of the romance and a bit of the *neshuma* (soul) of the Lower East Side was gone forever.

New York City's Multiple Dwelling Law of 1929 was intended to improve living conditions in the tenements, but many landlords simply abandoned their properties because they realized that no matter how much they raised rents, they'd never be able to recoup the money they would have to spend to bring their decrepit buildings up to the new code. Other landlords kept their buildings unoccupied, allowing them to fall into further disrepair as they awaited the long-delayed buyouts from the city government as part of the slum clearance process.

Between 1910 and 1940, the Lower East Side experienced a 60 percent decline in population. Those who remained were, for the most part, the worst off. The saddest, however, were people like the Russ family, who had left the Lower East Side but had to move back to the neighborhood because the financial reversals they experienced during the Great Depression meant that they could no longer afford to live in those coveted homes in the outer boroughs.

The Daughter of Tanenbaum the Baker, the Wife of Leo the Butcher

One day about a year ago, Ruth Tanenbaum Shapiro appeared in the store and introduced herself to Niki. She was, she said, "the daughter of Tanenbaum the baker" (181 East Houston Street) and "the wife of Leo the butcher" (175 East Houston Street). She hadn't been to the old neighborhood for years. Realizing that Ruth might be a gold mine of Lower East Side history and information, Niki got me on the phone, and Ruth and I set up a date to talk so she could fill in some of the blanks in my research for this book.

On the appointed day, the store was filled with customers, but eighty-seven-year-old Ruth Tanenbaum Shapiro ("Call me Ruthie") was easy to pick out of the crowd. When I offered to pay Ruthie back for her cab ride from her apartment on the Upper West Side, she said, "What cab? I came by subway." When asked if she'd like to sit down and have something to eat, her response was "Maybe later."

Thirty minutes into our conversation, *I* needed to sit down and have something to eat. I opened two folding chairs in the front of the store near the herring showcase. We noshed a *bissel* halvah while she reminisced about life on the Lower East Side from the 1920s to the 1950s.

> Of course I knew your mother, Annie, and your aunts, Hattie and Idie. They worked in their father's store and I worked in my father's bakery, two doors away. If they were very busy, I would help them out and take herrings from the barrels and wrap them in newspaper for the customers.
>
> I began working in my father's bakery when I was six years old. We lived on the second floor, right above the store. Only my father and I knew how to make change. We sold bread for six cents a pound and rolls for a few pennies each. Where I live now, bread is three to four dollars a loaf and the rolls are seventy-five cents each. Can you believe it? Bread was delivered to us and came in one-, two-, four-, and eight-pound loaves for the rye, up to twelve pounds for the pum-

pernickel. We cut the big loaves in half and then cut a wedge from the half. The customer would show us with her hands how big a wedge she wanted. If someone was having a party and wanted sliced bread, I sliced it by hand with a knife. My father finally gave in and bought a slicing machine. The wheel was turned by hand. He didn't buy an electric slicer until much later. It was very loud and made the whole store shake. My father was a religious man, very conservative at home and in business. He didn't like to make changes.

One Sunday my mother was helping out in the store. She put her hand on the wrong side of the slicing machine and it cut off the tips of two fingers. I put her fingertips in a towel and rushed her over to Dr. Isaacs's home. Since he was a customer, I knew where he lived. He was the biggest doctor at Beth Israel Hospital. He was a surgeon and he would do all the important operations. He even operated on his own son. There were no specialists in those days. He would operate on all parts of the body: the head, the stomach, the feet. He was a bit *meshuggah* but the biggest, the best. So he let us into his house and he sewed on my mother's fingertips right there. A beautiful job. Like new. And he didn't charge us a dime. From everybody else he demanded payment in advance. After that, whenever he came into our store I dropped everything to take care of him. And if he wanted some fish from Russ next door, I would take him in and tell them to take care of him right away. Ask your mother and your aunt. They'll know him. Dr. Isaacs. Beth Israel. The biggest!

We also sold bagels and bialys. Bagels were three for a nickel. We had cakes—sponge, honey, cheesecake, *mun,* mandelbrot, and checkerboard—at fifteen cents a pound. Cookies, Danish, jelly doughnuts, and kichlach were twenty-five cents a pound. After shul, people would eat a piece of herring and a kichel instead of bread. If they ate bread they had to wash their hands, say the blessing over the bread, and then the blessing after. The kichlach were made with fruit juice and weren't considered bread, so they could avoid making the extra blessings. For breaking the fast on Yom Kippur we sold a lot of pumpernickel from Stumann's bakery. Stumann's was German, not Jewish; Jews weren't allowed to eat bread that had been baked by other Jews during the fast day.

Everything you needed was right on your block. On the corner was

Ershowsky's. They sold meats and poultry, but they were not kosher. In the window were trays of turkey tails; those were very popular. During holidays they cooked whole turkeys, twenty-five at a time, in a big gas oven at the back of the store. Each cooked turkey was carved on a machine; then the meat was put back on the frame and covered with the skin. You couldn't even tell it had been carved. They sold a lot of these turkeys to the unions, which gave them out as gifts. When a customer wanted a cut of fresh meat, she would put on a white butcher's coat and accompany the worker—they had fifteen people working in the store—into a big walk-in refrigerator with sawdust on the floor. The meat was hanging from big hooks and they cut it for the customer right there. Besides fresh meat, the store made and sold pickled tongue and corned beef, smoked pastrami, salami, and frankfurters.

Leo and Harry were two boys who worked for Old Man Ershowsky. The old man got tired and sold the store to them. I married Leo in 1946. My father, who was kosher, wasn't happy that his son-in-law sold *trayfe*. My father was concerned that people would think that he was eating *trayfe* from his son-in-law. But he liked Leo. Leo was a nice Jewish boy from the neighborhood, and he spoke a good Yiddish. What's not to like? After we got married, we moved in with Leo's mother on Second Street just across Houston, and we lived there for ten years until we moved uptown in the mid-1950s. I'm still in the same apartment at Central Park West and Ninety-second Street. I have eight rooms, with four bathrooms. It overlooks the park. I live there alone. Lots of people moved from the Lower East Side to Forest Hills, but Leo didn't want to commute too far. He worked all the time.

Next to Ershowsky's was Eisenberg's appetizing store. I think he worked for your grandfather for a while. Right next to your grandfather's place, in the same building, there was another commission bakery, Baskin's. They were like us but even smaller. Tillie Baskin wanted her son to marry my sister; it didn't happen. After Baskin's was your grandfather's store. Each morning Ivan rolled out the herring barrels to put on the street in front of the store. Your grandfather got Ivan from the Bowery. I remember the Russ girls, Hattie, Idie, and Annie. They were all very pretty. They worked very hard. We all worked hard. That's what we had to do in those days. I remember seeing your great-uncle with his long beard and black coat and hat. He would sit in the front of the store and watch. He was the watcher. My father once told me that before the girls came in full-time, your grandfather had two young men working in the store. They had pegged pants. My father said to your grandfather in Yiddish, "Russ, these boys will never let you make a living. You should bring your daughters into your business." And your grandfather said, "My daughters sell herring for a living? Never!" But then they did. And their husbands, too. [I ran this by Aunt Hattie, who doesn't remember anyone working behind the counter at that time other than Harry Eisenberg. And she says that her father always expected his daughters to come into the business. I guess everyone is entitled to a little literary license.]

In between your store and our bakery, there was a dairy store that sold eggs, milk, and butter. It was tub butter; they cut chunks of butter from a big block. Customers brought in their own bottles, and the milk was ladled out of a large metal can. Buttermilk was three cents a glass. And cheeses: farmer's cheese, pot cheese, American cheese; nothing fancy like now. Later on, they sold baked farmer's cheese with fruits and nuts and raisins.

On the other side of our store was a deli called Leibowitz and Klein that sold pastrami, corned beef, and tongue sandwiches and hot dogs. A sandwich was ten cents. Then it became Henry's, after the war, I think. When the landlord raised the rent, Henry moved his delicatessen to the next block.

On each street corner there were pickle vendors who sold sours, half sours, and pickled tomatoes from barrels. They paid rent to shopkeepers to store their pickle barrels at night. In the street in front of the stores there were pushcarts. I remember the pushcart directly in front of your store. The peddler sold onions and potatoes. No one could get over it when his daughter married a son of Yavarkovsky, the paper-goods dealer on Ludlow Street. Hoo-ha!

Across the street on the corner was a tiny candy store where you could get sodas with seltzer and different flavored syrups. They were the best sodas because the lady made the syrups herself. Next to the candy store was a mushroom store. Everyone used mushrooms in those days. Mostly for soups. And next to the mushroom store was a dairy restaurant, Shwebel's, where you could get blintzes, pierogi, soup, and fruit with sour cream. And on the corner of Ludlow and Houston was Katz and Tarowsky's delicatessen. [It's now known as Katz's, but it is no longer owned by the original family.]

Around the corner on Orchard Street there was another appetizing store: Nathan's. Farther down Orchard, maybe between Stanton and Rivington, there was another one, Gartenberg's. His son wanted to be a doctor, but they weren't accepting many Jewish boys into medical schools in those days. So Gartenberg sent his son to Europe to school.

On Orchard Street there were lots of poultry stores. Most people bought a whole chicken and plucked the feathers themselves. If they wanted the poultry man to pluck the chicken, they had to pay an extra fifteen cents. And Orchard Street was filled with pushcarts. It wasn't fancy. It was the bottom. Clinton Street, that was a better street. They had fancier stores selling clothing; they were up-to-date.

When our talk was over, I offered to put Ruthie into a cab to go home.

"What cab? I don't need a cab. Don't waste your money. I'll go by bus. I'm from the old school."

The Dark-er-est Days

My cousin Marty says that one day in the late 1940s he was standing with Grandpa Russ outside the Russ & Daughters building, which Grandpa had just bought. He heard Grandpa say "Oy."

"What's the matter, Grandpa? Are you sorry you bought the building?"

"No," Grandpa replied. "I'm sorry I didn't buy more of them."

Grandpa, like many Eastern European Jews who were denied the right to own land in the Old Country, equated success with property ownership. He had no idea and did not foresee how bad things would get.

The 1950s brought a sea change of demographics to the Lower East Side. Over the course of the decade, most of the Jewish families, including the Russes, moved out of the neighborhood. Those who remained were either too poor to leave, too committed to their synagogues, or too attached to their elderly parents, who wanted only to live out their lives in the old neighborhood—whatever it was becoming. William Levitt was building suburban tract homes at low prices on Long Island. Robert Moses was building roads and highways that made it easy to commute to them. And the federal and state governments financed everything. The New York City rent control laws of 1943 were designed to protect tenants from excessive rent increases. Instead, the laws drove more landlords to abandon properties; there was no point in making costly repairs or renovations if they couldn't increase rents. Those who kept their tenements began to replace the departing Jews with new arrivals to the city—blacks, Puerto Ricans, and Dominicans. Where large tracts of tenement slums were torn down, low-income public housing projects were erected.

A few newly created islands of middle-class life offered some stability. Not-for-profit, cooperative-style high-rise apartment buildings were built along Grand Street and East Broadway, with funds from unions such as the Amalgamated Clothing Workers and the International Ladies' Garment Workers' Union, and the support of the federal and state governments. They were intended for the benefit of union workers, but as inexpensive as this subsidized housing was, it was still too costly for most of them. For the most part, the apartments in those buildings were filled with merchants and professionals who had grown up in the tenements and couldn't bring themselves to abandon the neighborhood. But the lion's share of federal, state, and city funds went toward the construction of low-income housing projects. The dreams of Grandpa Russ and his fellow merchants to have the neighborhood become a bedroom community for Wall Street and the Financial District came to nothing.

While many local merchants moved their families out of the neighborhood, they held on to their stores because their customers continued to come back to shop, especially on the weekends. The Sunday blue laws, which restricted retail shopping on Sundays throughout the state, specifically exempted Lower East Side shops. This was the lifeline for neighborhood merchants. On Sundays there were often long lines outside Orchard Street's discount handbag, designer clothing, and underwear shops. Uptown and out-of-town women waited to get into some of the stores, and once in, they got right into the spirit of the neighborhood as they tried on the latest fashions in the back of stores that had never heard of dressing rooms. Then they walked over to Grand Street to stock up on linens, towels, slipcovers, curtains, and other dry goods. Bargains abounded on the Lower East Side.

And after all that shopping, the bargain hunters had to get something to eat. Perhaps something dairy—blintzes, mushroom barley soup, kasha varnishkes, or latkes—at Ratner's, Galishoff's, or the Grand Dairy. Or maybe some deli—a hot dog, a corned beef or pastrami on rye, a salami or a tongue sandwich—from Katz's, Henry's, Crown, or Bernstein's. Then over to Russ & Daughters, Scotty's, J&J, or Saperstein to take home some herring and lox. Throughout the 1950s and '60s there were still lots of choices for shoppers. Today, only Katz's, Russ & Daughters, and Yonah Schimmel on Houston Street, and Noah's Ark on Grand Street remain.

In the 1970s, the advent of the suburban mall with its huge parking lots, enclosed climate-controlled shopping, and fast-food outlets meant that the customers could trade in their nostalgic shopping trips to the Lower East Side for convenience. In 1976 the Sunday blue laws ended, allowing retailers everywhere to be open on Sundays. The first department store to take advantage of this change was E. J. Korvette, one of the original discounters of appliances and other items. This was the final blow for the merchants of the Lower East Side. Fewer and fewer customers came to the neighborhood. Some shopkeepers relocated their stores to the suburbs to be closer to their customers. But if they had grown old and tired in their stores and had no "next generation" to take over, they simply closed their businesses and moved to Florida.

"Why don't you move your business uptown, where your customers are?" I was often asked during this period.

My standard reply: "Sooner or later, uptown will move downtown."

It was just a response. I didn't believe the neighborhood would ever change. So why didn't we move our shop uptown or out of Manhattan? Because we owned the building, and moving would mean paying rent to a "stranger." The unchallenged truth in the Russ family: "Once a landlord sees you doing business, he wants to become your partner." And I knew in my *kishkes* (guts) that we were historically in our rightful place in the world. Would a herring really taste like a herring if it was bought on the Upper East Side or in Great Neck?

Although the low-income public housing built in the 1950s and '60s did clear away the worst of the slums, it didn't solve all of the problems of this new generation of poor immigrants. Light manufacturing was disappearing from New York, the municipal government was cutting back on its blue-collar jobs, and the departure of the small businesses further depleted the working-class job pool. It wasn't hard to figure out that crime would soon follow, and it did. Then came the drug dealers, who openly sold their wares in the empty lots and abandoned tenements to both local residents and users who came from all over the city.

During the 1970s and '80s, the neighborhood looked like a war zone. The storekeepers who stayed hunkered down and installed solid, roll-down metal security gates so that no one could look inside. Russ & Daughters installed gates with a see-through diamond-shaped pattern so passersby could look into the store when it was closed. It wasn't like we were selling designer shoes or handbags. Who would want to break into a fish store?

Customers who still came to shop on the Lower East Side had their cars broken into because they had left a briefcase on the front seat or a radio in the dashboard; this was an engraved invitation to a junkie needing a fix. To combat shoplifting and pickpocketing, we created a code so as not to frighten the customers: "Two-ten!" an employee would shout. That meant keep your two eyes on the ten fingers of the unsavory-looking type standing too close to the pocketbook of the well-dressed lady from the Upper East Side who's too busy watching her salmon being sliced to notice him. The bocce court across the street—formerly a favorite spot for Italians from nearby Little Italy—had turned into a "needle park" where junkies met their pushers. The prostitutes over on Chrystie Street picked up their johns and took them to the abandoned "trick house" a few doors away from our store, or serviced them right in the guys' cars parked on the street. Occasionally a hooker, her sheepish-looking john in tow, would come into the store to get change for a hundred-dollar bill so she could get paid her ten bucks. Sometimes the same john would come flying into the store a few minutes later, hysterical, wanting to know if we saw his "date," because she took the other ninety dollars while he was sleeping. We got to know some of the local hookers, who would buy candy from us. They all seemed to have a sweet tooth.

Despite the petty crimes and graffiti, Russ & Daughters remained relatively unscathed by the crime that pervaded the neighborhood. The one big theft we had was an inside job: a considerable amount of money was stolen by one of our employees, someone whom I had considered a trusted worker for many years. After that I became a true New York cynic, both to the world outside and the world inside our little store. But Russ & Daughters stayed put.

Some neighborhood merchants were not so fortunate. One well-known longtime Orchard Street leather-goods shop had two partners. Partner A had two sons, the older of whom he took into the business. That son couldn't get along with partner B and opened his own store across the street. The younger son became a drug addict, readily supplied by the neighborhood pushers. Over the years, we watched as the young man's addiction worsened and the father's many expensive attempts to have him cleaned up in rehab failed. The father created an account with us so that his son could come in and buy something to eat: a bagel and lox, maybe some sturgeon every once in a while. We had to tell his father that this wasn't working. The son charged fancy and expensive canned goods, olive oils, and jars of caviar to sell on nearby streets and then used the proceeds for a fix. After several years, the father's persistence seemed to pay off. The son returned from another trip to rehab, and this time he was clean. He dressed in suits and ties, put on some weight, and spoke in complete and lucid sentences. The father was pleased and took the son into his business. All seemed to be going well. Then, one night while I was watching the evening news, I saw the son in a "perp walk." He had hired a hit man to kill partner B. The hit man, however, was an undercover cop. Not long after his arrest, the son died in jail. The leather-goods store, a beloved shopping destination featured in many guidebooks, eventually closed.

With the housing projects bursting at the seams and no money available for any kind of new construction, during the 1970s and '80s few people moved into the neighborhood by choice. As always, it was housing of last resort. With one interesting exception. The young artists, writers, and musicians who had been priced out of Greenwich Village as it became gentrified and went from an affordable counterculture space to an expensive yuppie neighborhood began to scout out the Lower East Side. Attracted by the cheap rent in the tenements and the few run-down brownstones that were still habitable, they were also intrigued by the neighborhood's edgy lifestyle. Small stirrings of commerce began to be seen. Hilly Kristal loved to come by to treat himself to bagels and lox and schmooze with me about the evolving local music scene. In 1973 he had turned his Bowery bar into CBGB, a country, bluegrass, and blues club, but shortly thereafter it morphed into a legendary punk rock mecca.

In the 1970s you could buy any tenement building on the Lower East Side for $25,000. But no one was buying. Some abandoned tenements were taken over by squatters, who called themselves "urban homesteaders." In many cases, the squatters did improve their buildings and the immediate surroundings, but their illegal occupancy often led to confrontations with the police and the courts. The most famous was the Tompkins Square riot of 1988. This took place several blocks away from us, but it spilled over into our neighborhood. Rioters raced by our store, yelling, "Die, yuppie scum!" I tried not to take it personally.

Somehow, I continued to run the store in this environment. I woke up early each morning, slid open the metal gates, made sure the right fish got into the store, saw to it that the employees showed up, and then hoped that customers would, too. Jewish merchants from the neighborhood liked to come in, have a bite to eat, and *kvetch* about how bad things were. Their children were "established," and there was no reason for them to continue in business. They'd say, "I need this like a *lokh in kup* [hole in the head]." Sometimes, as they reached across the counter to take the *shtickel* herring I offered, a shirtsleeve would ride up, revealing numbers tattooed on a forearm. These neighbors knew about suffering. They could complain to me all they wanted.

The '90s: Renaissance and Renovation

By the mid-1980s, the expanding economy began to bring changes to the equally distressed East Village, the neighborhood of numbered streets just north of Houston Street and west of Alphabet City (as Avenues A through D came to be known during the dark times in the 1970s). Once historically part of the Lower East Side, the East Village had acquired its own real estate appellation in the 1960s as it became the destination of choice for New York's flower-child population. Buildings were being bought up and gloriously rehabilitated, and young professionals (yes, those notorious "yuppie scum") were starting to move in. It would take another five to ten years before gentrification began to make any serious inroads on the Lower East Side south of Houston. For a while it appeared to be a race between the Chinese developers, who began moving eastward and northward from Chinatown (with, word on the street had it, "suitcases full of cash"), and developers from outside the neighborhood.

By the 1990s changes on the Lower East Side were apparent. Max Fish opened on Ludlow Street in 1989, leading the way for a neighborhood bar and club scene, a hangout for local artists, musicians, and writers. It's now on the verge of closing, its owners unable to afford the skyrocketing rent that this now prime real estate commands.

Rosario's Pizza, on East Houston since 1963, lasted as long as it did because of the hard work and long hours proprietors Phillip and Sal Bartolomeo, a father-son team from Sicily, put in. They were forced to leave their forty-year location to make room for fast-food operators. Shastone Monuments, which provided the headstones for many Russ family members at Beth David Cemetery, is now home to the Mercury Lounge, a bar and music venue.

Perhaps the best time line for understanding the changes in the neighborhood is the story of Ratner's Dairy Restaurant, a Delancey Street legend. Family owned and operated, Ratner's traced its roots on the Lower East Side to the early 1900s. By the 1970s, Ratner's was mostly serving those who had moved away but came back to shop and eat. But by the 1990s there were few Jews living in the neighborhood, and even fewer coming back for a visit. The Harmatz family, third-generation owners of Ratner's, saw the writing on the wall. They leased out space in the back of the restaurant, which became a trendy pseudo-speakeasy called—with a gangster-chic nod to neighborhood history—Lansky Lounge. (Gangsters Meyer Lansky and Bugsy Siegel were apparently both Ratner's and Russ & Daughters customers.) As the dairy restaurant business decreased, Lansky's expanded, taking over more and more of the restaurant space until it occupied all of it and became known as Lansky Lounge and Grill. But ultimately the power of real estate won out, and the Harmatz family sold the property to a developer who built a huge blue steel-and-glass condominium that now somewhat incongruously dominates the Lower East Side skyline.

Meanwhile, I continued to run Russ & Daughters, somewhat oblivious to what was happening around me. I was, however, very aware that our store—and I—were becoming increasingly old and tired-looking, much like the neighborhood. I had been fearful of making any changes, even minor ones. I was afraid of disappointing or discomfiting the regular customers who expected the store to look and feel a certain way, for each product to be in a particular place in the showcase: chubs in between whitefish and baked salmon, the schmaltz herrings in front of the matjes with rollmops in the middle. It had taken almost two decades for the customers to finally get used to me as the proprietor—even though I was a bona fide third-generation Russ—so I was reluctant to change anything else.

But by 1995 even I could tell that dramatic changes were under way on the Lower East Side. The store was busier. I would look up from slicing lox and see a well-heeled, well-educated crowd of younger shoppers. Expensive baby strollers replaced old wire shopping carts. These customers didn't buy many hard candies, but they did purchase fancy hand-dipped chocolates. And along with cream cheese, they also wanted sheep- and goat-milk cheeses to accompany their smoked salmon.

A renovation of the "candy side" was called for. And while we were at it, the linoleum floor and fluorescent lighting would go. The new candy-side showcase would have to accommodate the new upscale products. But I was determined that the renovation retain the look of a traditional appetizing store on the Lower East Side, and not turn Russ & Daughters into a soulless Upper East Side or SoHo eatery. I hired a business consultant, who in turn hired an architect, who in turn hired an engineer. I insisted that the look and feel of the store not change, and that all of the work, from beginning to end, take place within the two-week period when we would be closed for summer vacation. We achieved the desired results in almost the allotted time frame. It turns out, however, that making something look old costs twice as much as making it look new.

Having successfully renovated part of the store, why not renovate the entire building? It only took another five years and a lot of pressure from my wife to get started. Maria, like Grandpa Russ, believed in the power of real estate. But emptying the building of its residents, all of whom were our employees and their families, took time. For the previous twenty years, I had allowed some of our employees to live in the building, in the apartments above the store, almost rent-free but paying for heat. This arrangement worked for everyone. I had happy employees who didn't have to spend time and money commuting. (And there were no excuses that the subways were delayed.) They were so happy with the deal that they heeded the part of the Bible that commands "Be fruitful and multiply." Soon they and their families went from occupying a few apartments to occupying a few floors to eventually occupying the entire building. It was part of the deal that when I decided to renovate the building, they would have to move. Helping them relocate took several years.

The renovation was estimated at a cost of a million dollars, including a 10 percent cost overrun to do additional work that would preserve some of the building's historic details. The federal government had just declared the Lower East Side a National Trust historic district. It seems that the Lower East Side has the highest concentration of tenement buildings in the country, and someone who was awake at the federal level recognized that this was worth preserving. There was no mandate to restore historic architectural details, but the feds made a tax credit available for those who chose to participate. Unfortunately, they also created something called the AMT, an acronym for "alternative minimum tax" or, simply put, "Forget about the tax break you thought you had." Although the tax mathematics didn't work for me, I opted into the preservation program for emotional reasons. I was born on the Lower East Side, a block away from the store, and I wanted the store to remain part of its history. I couldn't bring myself to follow the trend of faux-marble façades that was all the rage.

The building renovation took two years and was completed in early 2001. We quickly rented the upstairs apartments to bankers, designers, and even a supermodel, who paid rents that would have been unimaginable to my grandfather and my parents, aunts, and uncles. After the horrific tragedy of September 11, 2001, several of our tenants lost their jobs or their desire to live in New York City, and they moved. To keep the remaining tenants and to replace those who left, we reduced rents and gave concessions.

It took a few years for the city to recover from 9/11. But when it did, the neighborhood began to experience a housing shortage and a building boom unlike anything we had ever seen. The Lower East Side was just too perfectly situated between uptown and downtown. The vision Grandpa Russ and his cronies had of the Lower East Side as a fancy-schmancy neighborhood was, more than half a century later, finally realized: high-rise condominiums, refurbished brownstones, boutique hotels, art galleries, designer clothing shops, national chain stores, and trendy restaurants have taken over the neighborhood.

These days, when visiting the store I often sit on the bench outside and take in the neighborhood. In the little park across the street where junkies and dealers did their business, kids play on swings and jungle gyms or run through the sprinklers while their mommies or daddies watch over them with one eye and read on their iPads with the other. The people who now use this park and live in this neighborhood are media consultants, graphic and fashion designers, computer experts, and bankers. They are celebrities and wealthy businesspeople who can afford to live anywhere they want, but they live in our little corner of the world. It turns out that I was right after all: uptown has moved downtown. With a vengeance. The Lower East Side, for more than one hundred years the place everyone wanted to leave, has become a place where people want to come to settle—if they can afford it. Somewhere, Grandpa Russ is smiling.

Egg Cream

SERVES 1

½ cup chilled whole milk
¾ cup or more chilled seltzer
3 to 4 tablespoons Fox's U-Bet chocolate syrup

Pour the milk into a tall soda or pint glass. Place a long spoon in the glass. Pour enough seltzer into the glass to come 1 inch from the rim (the mixture will foam). Pour the chocolate syrup in the center of the foam and stir until blended. Remove the spoon through the center of the foam.

Cheese Blintzes

MAKES 12 TO 14 BLINTZES, ENOUGH FOR 6 PEOPLE

CREPES
2 cups whole milk
4 large eggs
1⅓ cups all-purpose flour

FILLING
1½ pounds farmer's cheese
½ cup plus 2 tablespoons sugar
1 teaspoon pure vanilla extract
½ teaspoon cinnamon
Unsalted butter

To make the crepes, combine the milk, eggs, and flour in a food processor and process until smooth. Transfer the batter to a bowl and let it rest for 30 minutes. Meanwhile, prepare the filling. Combine the farmer's cheese, sugar, vanilla, and cinnamon in the work bowl of a food processor and process until smooth. Transfer to another bowl and set aside.

Melt a pat of butter in a heavy 8-inch nonstick skillet.* Ladle in just enough batter to coat the bottom of the skillet. (Tilt the skillet to coat it evenly.) Allow the crepe to cook undisturbed until it is set and the bottom is golden brown, 3 to 4 minutes. Loosen the crepe around the edges with a spatula and carefully transfer it to a paper-towel-lined plate. Repeat with remaining batter. You should have enough for about 14 crepes.

Spoon about 4 tablespoons of filling down the center of each crepe. Fold in the short ends and then roll up, burrito-style. Serve the blintzes immediately or rewarm in a 250°F oven.

**It's very important to use a nonstick skillet!*

6

The Products

What We Sell

When I decided to stop practicing law and go into the family business full-time, I asked my father to teach me how to tell a good fish from a bad fish. "No problem," he said. "I'll teach you the same way your grandfather taught me. First, we'll go to the smokehouses and you'll watch how I look at, feel, and taste the fish. Then, when we get the fish into the store, you'll watch how the fish are laid out in the walk-in box so they get the circulating air but are kept free of moisture. You'll help me select which fish go into the showcase first, always rotating the stock so that first in is first out. Then, when you're waiting on a customer, you'll be handling the fish again and you'll be feeling the texture as you move the knife through it. You'll offer the customer a taste, but most of the customers will say, 'You taste it'; they want your assurance that this piece of fish is perfect. Even if only one of their guests complains, you'll hear about it the following week: 'What kind of fish did you pick for me last week? Did I have to be embarrassed in front of my company?' You'll see how the taste and texture change as you slice up the length of the fish from tail to head. Then, after ten years, maybe you'll know how to tell a good piece of fish from a bad one."

Soon after this conversation took place, my father was forced by ill health to retire. Not long after that, he died. Since I'd had few opportunities to go with him to the smokehouses, I was left on my own to learn how to buy fish from his former cronies, the fish smokers.

These first-generation Americans joined or took over their family businesses when they returned from duty after World War II. By the time I entered the business in 1978, they had become the old-timers. They walked around their fiefdoms with permanent scowls on their faces and cigars stuffed in their mouths, saying very little. And what they did say was usually designed to intimidate retailers like me.

Even in the late 1970s, fancy lake sturgeon was in short supply. Since sturgeon feed off the bottoms of rivers and lakes, the fish often has a distinct, unpleasant muddy flavor that remains even when it is smoked. Retailers want only the clean, sweet-tasting fish with lines of yellow fat running through the flesh. These pieces of fish are known as "candy."

Jack, the sturgeon keeper at one of our primary suppliers, was a shrewd businessman. To get candy sturgeon I had to plead, beg, and grovel. But even that wasn't enough. If I wanted twenty pounds of candy sturgeon, I also had to buy one hundred pounds of salmon, whitefish, or whatever other fish he had too much of.

The wholesale smoked-fish industry, originally the province of German immigrants, became primarily owned and run by Eastern European Jewish immigrants in the 1920s. They made several efforts to bring what were understood to be "American business practices" (i.e., monopolization and restraint of trade) into the industry. When product and market manipulation, price gouging, and the threat of strikes failed, they used coercion, extortion, and other strong-arm tactics to get their way.

When I was a kid, I would hear at family gatherings the occasional mention of someone called "Lobster." His name was spoken in the whispered tones usually reserved for a relative recently diagnosed with cancer. Sigmund Einstoss, aka Lobster, was the primary focus of an investigation into the smoked-fish industry by the New York State Attorney General's office in 1926. It was alleged that he attempted to control the industry by making his competitors join his trade association or be driven out of business. Some who resisted were, in fact, put out of business; others were beaten up. Lobster wound up controlling the supply of smoked fish to distributors and then drove up the prices to retailers by more than 100 percent, sending smoked whitefish from eighteen cents to forty cents a pound. In 1938, a New York State commission charged many of the smoked-fish distributors with using threats, intimidation, and illegal picketing in an attempt to force retailers to buy from their association. In 1944, another investigative commission led to indictments and jail sentences for smokers who had violated wartime price controls. In 1955, a federal criminal indictment and separate antitrust suit was filed against many New York–area smokers who conspired to eliminate competition. Dealing with smokehouses and smokers was a dirty, fishy business in many ways. Still, business had to go on, and Russ & Daughters depended on these suppliers for our products. Several of the defendants in these lawsuits attended my bar mitzvah in 1958.

My early years dealing with the smokers were humbling as well as humiliating. I may have been a lawyer, but to them I was still a kid. They couldn't believe that I had willingly given up a professional career to work in the fish business. Hadn't they all worked so hard so that their children could become lawyers and doctors? It occurs to me now

Grandpa Russ and me at my bar mitzvah, in 1958. That was probably how the smokers saw me in 1978, as well.

that seeing what they perceived to be my professional failure may have stoked their fear for the security of their own kids. So they weren't going to make this process easy for me. No free ride for the third generation of the Russ family. Often they tried to game me by seeing if I would buy or reject bad fish they slipped into a pile.

The process of selecting fish is complicated. You need four of your five senses, all operating at the top of their form. *Smell:* A bad fish lets you know it's bad, that it's past its prime, even before you have laid eyes on it. It has an off-putting smell that makes you wish you had a cold. *Sight:* It is expected, even appreciated, that the colors of fish, particularly wild fish, vary greatly. But some color issues are disqualifiers. Bruises and blood spots on the sides of smoked salmon indicate that the fish may have been abusively caught and may have thrashed around in a seine net for days. Yellowing on the belly area may be evidence of "freezer burn." Uniform, bright, Day-Glo colors might be attractive but suggest the presence of chemical dyes. *Feel:* How the fish feels in your hand will translate into how it feels in the mouth, that is, its texture. By touching the fish ever so gently, you should be able to identify and reject those fish that are undercured or overcured, to tell whether the fish is fresh or has been frozen, and to determine whether it will be tough or tender, firm or mushy. *Taste:* Finally, the trained purveyor should have developed a palate that will confirm that these fish, which have passed all other sensory tests, are worthy of sale to consumers. The smoke should be naturally rich and deep, not sharp and tasting of chemicals, and the salt should be balanced throughout the fish and should enhance rather than mask the flavor.

It took me about five years to become a true smoked-fish expert and to earn the fish smokers' respect. I was relieved that it hadn't taken the ten years my father had predicted. When Niki and Josh came into the business, their internships were five years as well.

The Herring Pairing

What would Grandpa Russ have thought about this event? He arrived in America in 1907 and began selling herring for five cents apiece from a pushcart on the Lower East Side. Now look what his great-grandchildren had come up with.

"Who the hell is going to pay sixty-five dollars to eat herring for three hours? Are you crazy? Your great-grandfather must be rolling over in his grave." That was my response when I was first told by Niki and Josh about the Russ & Daughters Herring Pairing, an event that was created to be an annual celebration of the arrival of the season's first catch of Holland herring. "And what the hell is a herring pairing, anyhow?"

"Dad, you just don't get it," sighed Niki. "It's not just about herring." I have to admit I didn't get it at first. "And by the way," she added, as proof that I didn't know what I was talking about, "we're already sold out." Niki and Josh loved to point out that I had become a dinosaur in this business. Here was a perfect example.

On an early summer evening several years ago, three hundred people gathered at the Astor Center, a culinary arts venue in Lower Manhattan, where they paid sixty-five dollars per person to sample eight different types of herring, each paired with specially selected vodkas, whiskeys, and other more exotic spirits.

Chef Wylie Dufresne, famous for his molecular cooking, created a soup made from herring frozen with liquid nitrogen and then pulverized; he garnished the soup with nasturtium flowers. Composer, musician, and performer John Zorn played his original compositions of New Age klezmer music. Individual tables were set up to display each of the various herrings: schmaltz, matjes, and rollmops; herring pickled in cream sauce, in wine sauce, in curry sauce, and in mustard and dill. There was an ice sculpture (in the shape of a fish, of course) on which the first-of-the-season Holland herrings were displayed. A photographer was taking sepia-toned portraits for those who wanted a memento of the evening. And the Russ family was there to serve and to schmooze. The crowd was a mix of celebrities from the art, literary, and culinary worlds; most were longtime or enthusiastically new Russ & Daughters customers. No tourists, no curiosity-seekers. This was an event celebrating herring, Russ & Daughters, and New York itself. And there I was, watching three hundred people sliding herrings down their throats with the gusto of sea lions being fed at Sea World. It was beautiful. Everyone there was happy to share the evening, the food, and their stories.

Perhaps out of need but more likely out of guilt, Niki gave me an assignment for the evening: I would speak to groups of thirty attendees at a time culled from the main crowd. I was to do this three to four times during the evening. I should not be "too preachy, or too schmaltzy," Niki instructed. "Keep it short, maybe fifteen to twenty minutes for each presentation. And light, not too much information. Be informative but don't be long-winded. You know what to do, Dad." I was flattered by her trust in me, but, actually, I didn't. Although the Russ family has been selling herring and smoked fish for more than one hundred years, a celebrity-filled, media-friendly herring-pairing event was not part of the family tradition as handed down by Grandpa Russ.

While talking to the first group of guests, I saw their eyes glaze over and their hands furtively checking iPhones as I lectured on the life cycle and mating habits of *Clupea harengus,* the North Atlantic herring species. To regain the attention of my audience, I dropped the herring biology lesson and instead told the story of our family: how herring brought Grandpa Russ to America; how his three pretty daughters had to sell herrings in his store rather than go to college; how their husbands were expected to do the same; how they worked six and seven days a week, ten to twelve hours a day, so that their children wouldn't have to sell herring for a living; how the store remained on the Lower East Side when most of the customers had moved away and the neighborhood spiraled into despair; and how well-educated members of the third and fourth generations worked in other professions before feeling the emotional tug of the family business and returning to carry on the Russ family traditions. Suddenly, I had everyone's attention. My presentation was a hit.

The evening's great success made a simple statement that everyone who attended recognized: No matter how the world around us is changing, there is something lovely and meaningful about people getting together to share a food experience, and there is something special about a family that is dedicated to sharing their herring products and their lives with others. There will always be herring to sell on the Lower East Side, and there will always be a Russ around to sell it.

I think—no, I'm sure—that Grandpa Russ would have *kvelled* at this evening's event, because it was herring that had brought him to America, herring that enabled him to provide for his family, and herring that made his customers happy.

In Danish, herring is called *sild.* In Swedish, *sill.* In French, *hareng.* In German, *Hering.* In Italian, *aringa.* In Spanish and Portugese, *arenque.* In Polish, *sledz.* In Russian, *seld.* In Greek, *righa.* In Turkish, *ringa.* And in Japanese, it's *kadoiwaski.* Most cuisines have some version of herring in their culinary lexicons. Herring is adaptable and versatile, lending itself to various food preservation techniques—salting, drying, smoking, pickling, and even burying it in the ground. And it can be prepared in a multitude of ways: chopped, fried, baked, pickled, and immersed in sauces.

Throughout the world, eating herring and smoked fish at a gathering of friends and family is not uncommon. The Jews call it *forshpeis,* the Swedes call it *smörgåsbord;* both mean "appetizers." Sometimes the herring cultures cross paths.

From Humble Herring to Haute Cuisine

In the early 1990s I received several invitations to dine at the Swedish consulate on the Upper East Side. The consul and his wife, extremely charming people, were promoting Swedish products in the United States, and they were eager to have some of their fish and cheese products sold in our store. Dinners at the consulate always began with starters of cheese, herring, aquavit, and song. I discovered that there were herring preparations beyond the pickled, schmaltz, matjes, and chopped versions available at Russ & Daughters. Until those dinners, I thought the only sauce for herring was cream sauce, but I soon became a fan of herring in curry sauce; in mustard and dill sauce; in sherry, ginger, and lemon sauce; and in tomato and fennel sauce.

I had long been thinking that herring deserved to be restored to its rightful place in the pantheon of fish. In Northern Europe herring played a role in the creation of political and economic alliances (the Hanseatic League, an alliance of cities and their merchant guilds, dominated trade from the thirteenth to the sixteenth centuries), caused wars (England vs. the Netherlands, 1652–54), and is used to this day in symbolic offerings to monarchs (the first herring of the season is formally presented each year to the Dutch royal family). I wanted to reverse the general disdain in which herring is held by second- and third-generation Jews. ("Ugh! Don't make me eat *herring*!") I had a dream that I could become the Ray Kroc of herring, that there would be McHerrings in every community. Millions of people would pass through the Arc de Herring.

At one of the consulate dinner parties I asked to meet the chef who had prepared the herrings. Out of the kitchen came Ulrika Bengtsson. She was dressed in her chef's whites, but she could easily have stepped out of a Swedish travel brochure: twentysomething, blond, and beautiful. Her personality was equally attractive: she was smiley, animated, and positive. There were lots of reasons to fall in love with Ulrika (professionally, of course), but my heart was forever hers when she prepared her family recipe of herring in parchment for me. (See recipe on page 86.) Potatoes, onions, and butter are layered between pickled herring fillets on parchment paper. The parchment packages are folded and crimped at the edges, placed on a baking sheet, and then baked for twenty minutes. Ulrika told me to stand directly over the parchment package when it was removed from the oven and opened. The aroma carried by the rising steam filled my nostrils and then headed directly into my soul. Ulrika may have been smelling her childhood in Sweden, but I was experiencing the aroma of my roots. In the early years of the last century, a Lower East Side housewife would buy a herring wrapped in newspaper, take it home to the tenement apartment, and then add potatoes and onions before putting it into the coal-fired stove. What emerged was dinner for the entire family.

I wanted to share my passion for herring with others. Soon the herring showcase at Russ & Daughters had not five but fifteen different herring preparations. We got newspaper and television coverage. During the Swedish Midsummer Festival, Ulrika, in traditional Swedish dress and with a garland of flowers in her hair, appeared on the Food Network to promote our herring products. When customers came to the store, I eagerly watched for their reactions to the new offerings and the expanded display. Their expressions ranged from disorientation to disdain. I stood behind the counter and offered samples, suggestions, and my *shpiel:* "Buy one of each and serve it to your guests on black bread or crackers. The Jews call it *forshpeis;* the Swedes call it *smörgåsbord.*" The most frequent customer response was "Interesting," which would be said flatly and without much conviction. They reluctantly tasted my offerings but bought the herrings they were used to: schmaltz, matjes, pickled in cream sauce, or chopped. I gave it six months and then reduced the fifteen herring offerings in our showcase to five. Ulrika went off to create her own eponymous restaurant on the Upper East Side.

Fast-forward to 2002, when the esteemed *New York Times* journalist R. W. ("Johnny") Apple Jr., who had retired from writing about international affairs, was traveling and writing about international foods. In an article titled "Herring, the Fish That Roared," he wrote about eating herring in Scandinavia. He advised readers who couldn't get to Norway or Sweden to visit "Ulrika's restaurant for a herring meal" and Russ & Daughters, "the city's herring-to-go headquarters." The power of *The New York Times* as the newspaper of record is legendary. And it turns out that this power also extends to shaping food tastes. Suddenly, the same customers who had chided me for stepping outside my traditional culinary boundaries were asking, "What happened to the herring in curry sauce you used to have?" We didn't become the McHerring sellers of my dreams, but Russ & Daughters did go back to selling more than five different types of herring and herring preparations. We increased it to ten, though, not back to fifteen. We do know our customers.

All Kinds of Herring: What's Not to Like?

In the beginning there was schmaltz herring. In German and Yiddish, *schmaltz* means "fat." The *Clupea harengus* from the cold waters of the North Atlantic were especially fatty, abundant, and suitable for preserving by submerging them in salt brine and packing them in large wooden barrels. (Due to health regulations, the barrels are now made of plastic, not porous wood.) From the 1600s to the 1900s, the Dutch and the British largely controlled the North Atlantic herring trade. Today it's Iceland and Norway. Nowadays the British are better known for their passion for kippers, salted and smoked herring that they eat with "bangers" (sausages). Oliver Sacks, the famous English neurologist, writer, and all-around genius, has said that his favorite meal is a schmaltz herring from Russ & Daughters. He was raised on schmaltz herring in England, where his father, a physician, ate them every day. This family was onto something. Unlike the fat in meat, which clogs the arteries, fish fat is high in cholesterol-lowering omega-3 fatty acids. This probably explains why on Sunday mornings Russ & Daughters is filled with cardiologists waiting to buy herring.

Schmaltz herring—salt-cured, barrel-stored fatty fish—not only became a staple on every Eastern European Jewish table as an inexpensive source of protein but also became a part of Jewish folklore, and even provided inspiration to some Jewish artists. When asked to describe his childhood, the Russian-born artist Marc Chagall said, "It smelled of herring." No wonder. His father worked in a salt herring factory. His mother stocked herring in her small grocery store. Herring even appears in some of his paintings, as flying fish. Now Marc Chagall's granddaughter is a Russ & Daughters customer. Across the counter, we have discussed the commonality of our ancestral roots: herring.

Matjes means "maiden," and it refers to young, pre-spawning herrings generally fished in the North Sea. The Swedes marinate them in brown sugar and cloves, which imparts a sweet-and-salty flavor. The Germans preserve them in vegetable oil, while the French prefer to smoke them and serve them over warm potatoes.

But the premier herring experience has to be the Hollandse Nieuwe. This is the spring catch of Dutch matjes herring, which is prized for its high-fat, low-salt content and its buttery texture. Traditionally, the Dutch auction off the first barrel of fish caught every year. The proceeds of the auction are donated to charity; the barrel of fish is presented to the Queen. Recently, the first barrel fetched €50,000, roughly $61,000. For all of its gastronomic glory, matjes herring is the street food of Amsterdam and other Dutch cities. Sold by vendors from stalls, it is served in a hot dog–style bun and covered with chopped egg and onion. A purist, however, will hold it by the tail and lower it into his or her open mouth.

Pickled herring follows Jews of European background from the cradle to the grave. Cut-up pickled herring fillets, smothered in cream sauce and onions, are often served at brises, baby namings, bar and bat mitzvahs, weddings, and funerals. Its versatility allows it to be accompanied by a wide variety of sauces: wine, cream, mustard and dill, curry. The origins of some of these sauces are cloudy. The Jews thought they had invented herring in cream sauce, but it was really the Swedes. The Swedes claimed to have invented herring in mustard and dill, but it was really the French. The Swedes did in fact invent *somstrumming.* No one else would have thought of it: canned herring buried in the ground and not eaten until the can is fully swollen. Getting past the smell is considered a Swedish rite of passage.

Displayed on a top shelf in the front of our store is an old piece of equipment. When I ask customers to guess its use, rarely do they get it right. It's an apple peeler/corer, used in bakeries for apple pies or strudel. At Russ & Daughters, it was used for three generations to core and peel apples for chopped herring salad. Granny Smith apples—the only kind to use, according to Grandpa Russ—impart a tart-tangy counterbalance to the sweetness of the pickled herring. We've been selling our old-fashioned chopped herring since the 1930s. Some consider it a spread and schmear it on rye or pumpernickel bread. Others serve it on a plate garnished with chopped hard-boiled egg and a dollop of sour cream, or with raw or pickled onions and boiled potatoes with chopped dill. However you serve it, chopped herring remains one of the true great noshes.

Bagels, Lox, and Cream Cheese

A Martian crash-lands his little spaceship at the corner of Orchard and Rivington Streets on the Lower East Side. When he climbs out, he sees that one wheel is missing. He decides to look for a replacement and notices a group of stores. As luck would have it, he passes a store that has a lot of appropriately sized wheels in the window. He goes inside. Moishe is at the counter.

"I would like to buy a wheel," the Martian says.

"We don't sell wheels," Moishe replies.

"Then what's that in the window?"

"Those are bagels."

"What do you do with them?"

"You eat them," Moishe says, offering one to the Martian. The Martian eats it and gives Moishe a big smile.

"Do you like it?" Moishe asks.

"It's good," replies the Martian. "But it would be even better with cream cheese and lox."

While this is not a great joke, I know, it's a joke that is now probably understood by the majority of people living in North America, regardless of their ethnic background. The bagel and its cream-cheese-and-lox counterpart have gone mainstream; they are now part of American culture.

Contrary to conventional wisdom, each part of this now-classic combination has its own separate history. The three components ultimately met and were married in the appetizing stores of the Lower East Side in the 1930s. At one time, every appetizing-store owner in the neighborhood claimed to be the originator of this creation. It has always been known as "bagel and lox"—the presence of cream cheese is understood. And there was no reason to use the word "sandwich"; what else could it be? Before the lox, cream cheese, and bagel troika came into being, smoked fish was traditionally eaten with butter schmeared on thick slabs of dark pumpernickel or rye bread. Which is still not a bad way to eat your smoked fish.

Salmon: Lox et Veritas

Confusion reigns when it comes to the difference between smoked salmon and lox. The word "lox" is derived from the German word *Lachs,* which means "salmon." The anglicized version, "lox," was first used to describe the millions of Pacific salmon caught, packed in a salt brine, and shipped to New York ports for further travels to Europe. Some of these fish found their way to Brooklyn smokehouses, where they were smoked in a heavy mixture of charcoal and wood chips. They were then sold in the appetizing stores on the Lower East Side, the "smoked lox" alongside the unsmoked salted salmon, known simply as "lox." Both products were extremely salty. The Eastern European Jews in the neighborhood had no prior experience in their shtetlach with salmon, smoked or otherwise, but they did bring with them a taste for salt-preserved fish like herring. Because huge quantities of salmon were available, the prices were very cheap—pennies for a quarter of a pound. Lox quickly caught on among the residents of the Lower East Side, and they took the taste for it with them when they moved out of the neighborhood.

Today there are many varieties of salmon available to consumers; they come from locations all over the world. What is known as New York–style smoked salmon is usually wet cured and cold smoked. In a wet cure the filleted sides of the salmon are dumped into large vats of salt water with a bit of brown sugar and left to soak for twenty-four to forty-eight hours. Europeans generally prefer a dry cure: salt is generously rubbed into the flesh of the salmon. The salt is rinsed off and the fish is then smoked. Whether dry- or wet-cured, salmon gets its silky texture from a cold smoking process, so called because the smoker gets no higher than 75°F. Industrial fans blow the charcoal-and-wood-chip smoke—often from cherry, apple, hickory, or oak trees—over the fish. Cold smoked fish has a delicate flavor and a silky texture, which allows for thin slicing. Hot smoking, by contrast, is an actual cooking process. The fish is brined and then smoked in an oven at a temperature of approximately 160°F. The fish flesh becomes flaky; it cannot be sliced thinly and gets chunked instead.

Every new customer at Russ & Daughters asks us the same question: "How much salmon should I buy?" It all depends on how you're serving it—on a bagel, on a slice of pumpernickel, or on a plate. Generally, two to three slices per bagel are sufficient. Allow two slices for a piece of pumpernickel, three to four slices on a bed of greens. Each slice should weigh about one ounce. Similarly, we are asked the best way to store and save any leftovers (there rarely are any). Smoked salmon sliced to order will last about a week to ten days in the refrigerator. To keep the salmon beyond that period, freeze it immediately after purchase. Defrost the fish gradually in the refrigerator for ten to twelve hours. If defrosted correctly, the salmon will retain its original taste and texture. If defrosted too quickly—in the microwave or at room temperature—the ice crystals will melt too fast, ruining both taste and texture.

Bagels and Cream Cheese: The Hole History

The origins of the bagel have always been a bit murky, but the generally accepted story places its beginnings in the late seventeenth century. A Viennese baker wished to honor Jan Sobieski, at the time the king of Poland and also a legendary military commander who in 1683 had saved the city from invading Turks. The baker fashioned a round roll with a center hole in the shape of Sobieski's stirrup, which in German is called a *Bügel,* and the bagel was born. More recently, a theory has been advanced that the bagel's origins are even older, going back to the thirteenth century in the Puglia region of Italy, where the local hard bread—a thin circle with a big hole in the center—is known as *taralli.* Located on the heel of Italy's boot, where the Ionian and Adriatic Seas come together, Puglia was a trade center, with merchants and merchandise traveling to and from Europe and the Middle East. At one time, Puglia had a substantial Jewish population. It's possible that when members of this community migrated to Eastern Europe, they brought the *taralli* with them, and that over time it became thicker and acquired a smaller hole.

The bagel landed in America along with the huge wave of Eastern European immigrants who began to arrive on the Lower East Side in the 1880s. Bagels were not difficult to make—they consist of flour, yeast, water, and salt—and once all the ingredients were combined, they were hand-rolled, boiled briefly in water, and baked in ovens located in the basements of tenement buildings. The finished bagels were displayed on sticks and sold on the streets for two cents apiece. A bagel was a quick, on-the-go snack, meant to be eaten by itself—an early form of fast food that was not originally intended to be the structural support for a sandwich.

The origins of cream cheese are equally cloudy. There are, of course, both French (seventeenth century) and English (sixteenth century) claims to its invention. The American version is traced back to a dairyman in upstate New York who, in 1872, was trying to reproduce the soft and creamy French Neufchâtel. His results were less fatty and less creamy but became a big hit when wrapped in silver foil and branded as "Philadelphia." (At that time Philadelphia, not New York, was an appellation of quality.) At Russ & Daughters we sell an all-natural cream cheese free of the chemical preservatives and stabilizers found in the commercially packaged products. We also sell, heaven help me, tofu cream cheese, for those who do not eat dairy products. And, frankly, it's not bad at all.

And That's How They Slice It?

You went salmon fishing in Alaska, caught a thirty-pound fish (no one ever catches a small one), had it smoked at a local smokehouse, and shipped it home. Or perhaps a friend sent you a whole Gaspé smoked salmon as a gift. Since freshly smoked fish isn't pre-sliced, how do you impress your friends and family with paper-thin slivers of salmon? Practice these steps and everyone will applaud your new Jewish sushi-chef skills.

First, you need the proper equipment: a sharp twelve-to-sixteen-inch knife with a flexible blade that is no more than two inches wide and tapers to a fine point; a pair of needle-nose pliers; and a cutting board.

Lay the salmon with the wider head end of the fish to your left and the narrower tail end to your right on a cutting board. (If you're a lefty, reverse the position.) You always start slicing at the head end, moving toward the tail.

Just as there are two ends (head and tail) to a salmon, there are also two sides. The thicker side is the loin; the thinner is the belly. Place the fish belly side up on the cutting board. There is usually a thin strip of fat that extends along the length edge of the belly side of the fish. Run the knife down this edge from top to bottom and remove that strip of fat. The knife will run into a small side fin (called *fliegel* in Yiddish); cut away the *fliegel* so that you will be able to remove it as part of the fat strip. If your knife skills are good, the thin strip of belly fat and *fliegel* will come away in one piece. (If not, ask friends to send more salmon to practice on.) Those in the know will eat this strip, since it's the richest, most succulent part of the fish. Native Alaskans call it "Eskimo candy." It's removed to make slicing easier, but it should be enjoyed, not discarded.

Sometimes there is a ribbing of bones that covers much of the belly side of the salmon. Slide the tip of the knife just under the top of the sheath of bones. Then slide the entire knife blade from the tip to the middle of the knife under the bone and down the side from the head to the tail to remove the layer of bone, leaving the salmon meat intact.

Gently run your fingertips along the top surface of the salmon to feel for any small pin bones, most often found in the middle of the fish. If you feel a bone, use the pliers to pull it out. It is important to remove all bones so the knife doesn't run into any obstructions when slicing. (And you don't want your guests suing you.)

Hold the knife firmly and think of it as an extension of your hand, not a separate tool. To slice, lay the knife blade almost totally flat—no more than a ten- to fifteen-degree angle—on top of the salmon. The top third of the knife blade is the only part that should be in contact with the fish. Your first slice will start at a point approximately six inches up from the tail of the salmon.

Slice—don't saw—with an easy back-and-forth motion, smoothly and evenly, at a consistent angle. Each slice must finish toward the tail end of the fish. Carefully pick up the slice in one hand and hold it up to the light; it should have the same even transparency throughout. If it breaks when you hold it up, then it was cut too thin. If the slice is entirely opaque, chop it up and add it to scrambled eggs and onions.

When slicing, it's important to maintain the same gentle pressure with each slice. Changing the pressure of your hand on the knife will create uneven, wavy slices. Work with the middle portion of the knife blade: the portion from one third down from the top to one third up from the bottom. Keep the knife as flat to the salmon surface as possible. In effect, you will be shaving off layers of meat, and the knife blade should be visible through the fish as you're slicing.

Caviar: Luxury on the Lower East Side

I recently found a letter in the office filing cabinet dated June 1969 from my father to a wealthy customer, advising her that the price for a pound of Russian beluga caviar was $69. (A Russian caviar pound is fourteen ounces.) Forty years ago, $69 a pound was considered a luxury. Today, in places where beluga caviar is still offered for sale (we were one of the first to take it off the menu years ago, when it became a threatened species), the price is about $250 an ounce, or $3,500 for a fourteen-ounce pound.

It is now common knowledge that the Russians overfished their sturgeon stocks and polluted their sturgeon-spawning rivers. What is less well known is that until about two hundred years ago, the United States had huge sturgeon fisheries along New York's Hudson River. The sturgeon meat was known as "Albany beef," and the salted sturgeon roe—caviar—was offered for free at local bars, along with a nickel beer. But we, like the Russians, failed to protect our waters and preserve our fisheries. The Convention on International Trade in Endangered Species (CITES) now controls the production, processing, importation, and sale of caviar, but it is too little, too late. The wild sturgeon species of the Caspian Sea—beluga, osetra, sevruga—have gone from threatened to endangered species, and the Hudson River no longer has a sturgeon fishery at all. Through the heroic efforts of conservationists, sturgeon are slowly starting to reappear in small numbers in the Hudson River.

When Caspian Sea caviar was readily available for sale in the United States (it was officially banned for sale here in 2005, under the Endangered Species Act; the ban was lifted to a limited degree in 2007), it was quite a challenge to establish and maintain relationships with caviar suppliers. Over the years, many of our suppliers ended up in jail, were on their way to jail, or were in hiding to avoid jail. Short supplies and high prices made this product "black gold." The ignorance of the consumer and the lack of enforcement of existing import and export regulations made it easy and financially rewarding for some suppliers to do the wrong thing: mislabel, bait and switch, buy smuggled products, freeze and sell old caviar. One supplier was indicted for selling American sturgeon roe as Russian beluga to a large airline that was serving it in first class. But he didn't wait around to be tried; he jumped bail and is now presumably in a country that doesn't have an extradition treaty with the United States. Another supplier, whose family for generations produced caviar for the czars, was indicted, convicted, and served jail time for his shady dealings.

I'm happy to report that the world of caviar has changed. Today it's all about sustainable farming of sturgeon and careful extraction and processing of the roe. Because this has proved to be so profitable, it is done in many countries throughout the world: France, Italy, Germany, the Czech Republic, Hungary, Romania, Spain, and Uruguay, to name a few. American fisheries have been involved in this for years, and *transmontanus,* a sturgeon native to California whose roe are similar to osetra in flavor and texture, has become a favorite of chefs throughout the world. The Chinese are now in the market with Kaluga, a *Huso* species similar to beluga, and *schrenkii,* which is similar to osetra. The Israelis are producing a beautiful golden osetra from the *Acipenser gueldenstaedtii* species. Not to be outdone, the Saudis are farming sturgeon, and next door Abu Dhabi is building what they claim will be "the largest caviar factory in the world."

It comes as a surprise to many people that the caviar produced from farm-raised sturgeon, no matter where in the world the farm is located, is very expensive: the prices generally range from $50 to $120 per ounce. This is because it takes a long time—up to eight years for some species—to raise the sturgeon to a point where the eggs are mature enough to be harvested. During that time, the fish must be fed and kept disease-free. Fortunately, there are affordable alternatives to sturgeon on the market. Paddlefish (a sturgeon look-alike) and hackleback (an actual member of the sturgeon family) are species found in the river deltas of the United States and are extremely good substitutes. They both look and taste like their more expensive sturgeon cousins and cost about $25 to $35 per ounce. Even more affordable are those big orange eggs from wild Alaskan salmon, the ones that "pop in your mouth" and sell for less than $5 an ounce, or French trout roe for about $7 per ounce. Consider topping your scrambled eggs with a dollop of sour cream and a big spoonful of salmon or trout roe.

Whether eating wild or farmed sturgeon roe, a great caviar experience means that the eggs taste as if the sea has kissed your tongue; they impart just the right amount of salinity to enhance, rather than mask, the underlying flavor. It is the retailer's responsibility to know by sampling the caviar supplied by the distributor which ones are worthy of sale to customers.

The visual criteria are straightforward: clean eggs of uniform size; no membranes or blood spots, which would indicate inferior processing; and eggs that easily separate rather than clump or stick together. (Old eggs clump together.) The color of the eggs is not an important factor in determining how the caviar will taste; it can vary from pale gray to dark black, or from dark yellow to bright gold, depending on the type of caviar. But eye appeal does add to the overall experience.

Determining whether the caviar you are buying tastes good is more difficult, since it relies on the subjective palate of the taster. Those of us who are serious purveyors of caviar have taught our palates how to taste. A tiny sample—no more than ten eggs—is placed on a mother-of-pearl spoon. (A metallic spoon, even one made of silver, will adversely affect both the taste and freshness of the caviar.) Each sample is tasted three times: first on the tip of the tongue for texture; then on the roof and back of the mouth for flavor; and then it's swallowed to check for any aftertaste—from the tin can, from mud or earth, or from too much salt. Between samples, the mouth is rinsed with lukewarm water.

The best advice: If you love caviar, find a reliable vendor with a reputation for integrity and for selling quality products. Someone who is selling what is being marketed as high-end caviar for a ridiculously low price is probably someone to stay away from.

I am often asked how much caviar one should buy. That all depends on how you intend to serve it. Some prefer the display of luxury and opulence that comes from serving caviar in its original tin, set in ice, or set in a crystal bowl or caviar server. After all, you are serving one of the world's greatest delicacies, so why not show off? If you allow guests to serve themselves, it's likely that you'll never have enough. To control the amount, make caviar canapés just before serving. One ounce per person is a very generous amount. Put a bit of caviar on a small square of white toast or on a blini and top with a dollop of crème fraîche.

Caviar can also be spooned into hollowed-out boiled new potatoes with a touch of sour cream on top. Then there are those (myself included) who prefer to eat it straight out of the tin, without anything else to get in the way of the pure caviar flavor. There are, of course, many ways to serve caviar, depending on your budget and your palate. The only mistake, and in my experience it's a common one, is to serve it with chopped egg and onion on top. If you have purchased good caviar, that would be, as we say in my neck of the woods, a *shanda* (shame).

Other Fish in the Sea (and the Showcase)

Half of the smoked-fish-eating world will swear that chubs are better than whitefish: they are, these folks claim, fatter, sweeter, less salty. The other half swears by whitefish for exactly the same reasons. Of the smoked-salmon aficionados, half will claim that the top half of the fish (nearest the head) is better; the other half make that same claim for the bottom half (by the tail). And so it goes in the world of smoked fish—and in food generally. Everyone is a maven. And who are we to take sides? We sell chubs and whitefish, salmon heads and tails. DE GUSTIBUS NON EST DISPUTANDUM (There is no arguing about taste) is the sign that hangs behind our cash register. It would be nice if there was a Yiddish equivalent that we could hang up alongside it, but the meaning in any language is clear: If you like it, it's the best.

CHUBS AND WHITEFISH: Those of us of a certain age (i.e., over fifty) and of a certain ethnic background (i.e., Jewish) will probably remember the look on our parents' or grandparents' faces when they were about to consume a chub or a piece of whitefish; it was something

Mushroom Barley Soup. See page 39 for the recipe.

Beet, Apple, and Herring Salad.
See page 104 for the recipe.

Left: Cheese Blintzes. See page 126 for the recipe.

Above: Whitefish Salad on Bagel Chips. See pages 157 and 190 for the recipes.

Above: Potato Latkes, topped with crème fraîche and caviar. See page 178 for the recipe.

Left: Bagel Pudding with Prunes and Raisins. See page 191 for the recipe.

Clockwise from top: Toasted bialy with kippered salmon, tomato, pepper, and capers; bagel with scallion cream cheese, Nova, and French trout roe; black bread with butter, sturgeon, and minced chives.

Flatbreads topped with pickled herring. *Clockwise from top left:* Pickled herring in cream sauce, schmaltz herring, pickled herring in wine sauce, curried herring, pickled lox, mustard-dill herring. See pages 135–37 for a more detailed explanation.

Facing page: A typical appetizing spread, ready for a family celebration.

This page: Smoked fish. *Top to bottom:* Whitefish, Nova, smoked Scottish salmon, gravlax, kippered salmon, sable, sturgeon, peppered mackerel. See pages 139 and 146–48 for a more detailed explanation.

Overleaf, clockwise from top: Chocolate-covered jelly rings and marshmallow bars, raspberry-and-walnut rugelach, black-and-white cookies, chocolate-covered marble halvah, assorted dried fruit, chocolate babka.

between intense focus and beatification. The fish was placed on a bed of lettuce accompanied by thick slices of tomato and onion; on the side would be a slice of either rye or pumpernickel bread, or a wedge of corn bread, or a toasted bialy. Butter was the preferred spread here, not cream cheese. With a knife and fork, the once-white skin of the fish, which had turned golden brown during the hot-smoking process, was peeled back to reveal the meat moistened by its own body fat. Boning the fish required the intensity and dexterity of a brain surgeon. There was no conversation, no kibitzing, just total focus as the meat slid away from the underlying layer of bones, leaving the fish frame intact. Then came the taste—rich, sweet, smoky, and satisfying.

The whitefish-and-chub experience is still available, but it is becoming increasingly rare. Their spawning and feeding grounds in the Great Lakes (their primary fishery) has been overrun by non-indigenous species such as the zebra mollusk and the lamprey eel, which were inadvertently introduced into the water through the ballast of ships that arrived from foreign ports.

STURGEON: Considered to be the crème de la crème of all smoked fish, sturgeon was a throwaway fish in the sixteenth and seventeenth centuries. It was so plentiful in the United States in the eighteenth and nineteenth centuries that it was exported to Europe, and even to Russia, along with its roe. But by the twentieth century, overfishing had turned sturgeon into an expensive delicacy. In the appetizing shops of the Lower East Side it commanded more than ten times the price of lox: when lox was being sold at thirty-five cents a pound in the 1920s and '30s, sturgeon went for $4 a pound. Aunt Hattie remembers that the wife of a very wealthy publishing magnate would frequent our store, arriving in a chauffeur-driven limousine. On each visit she would look at the price of the sturgeon in the showcase but never buy any. "I'm shocked! Too expensive!" she would loudly announce, as if to let the other customers know that although she was rich, she was still frugal. She would buy the cheapest thing in the store—sauerkraut. The smart shoppers in the neighborhood bought "sturgeon ends," the tips of the larger sturgeon pieces that would break off at the point where metal pins had been inserted to hang them for smoking. This part of the fish couldn't be sliced, so it was sold in small chunks. These small bits of sturgeon meat surrounding the bone were rich and delicious. Sturgeon ends sold for twenty-five cents a pound.

By the 1950s smoked sturgeon was considered such a delicacy that it figured in a Senate bribery investigation. In 1955 Harry Lev, a hatmaker from Chicago by way of Pinsk, Russia, was under investigation by the United States Senate's Permanent Subcommittee on Investigations for bribing government procurement officials to obtain a military hat contract. The alleged bribe: half a ton of smoked sturgeon. Harry's defense: a bribe is "something to wear, clothing"; sturgeon is something "very special to eat."

SABLE: Once called the "poor man's sturgeon," sable was presented to consumers as a replacement for carp, which was a common bony freshwater bottom-feeding fish whose muddy taste was masked with a mixture of paprika and garlic that was spread over the fish right before the smoking process. Sablefish, a black cod from the northern Pacific Ocean, was plentiful and cheap when it first entered the smoked-fish lexicon in the 1960s. It was prepared the same way as carp, but it had a much cleaner flavor and could be sold sliced from fillets and without bones. People preferred it over carp, and it became known to buyers and sellers as "chicken carp." But the Food and Drug Administration, in its wisdom, determined that this fish was neither chicken nor carp and disallowed use of the name. Thereafter, it was sold under its generic name, sablefish, or, more commonly, sable. Today, sable can no longer be called the poor man's sturgeon. The Japanese have discovered that black cod in sake-miso glaze suits their palates. They are the most voracious fish eaters in the world and will pay any price for their fish. So although it's still fairly plentiful, sable is no longer cheap.

The Disappearing Products: The Fish That Got Away

BUTTERFISH: Every so often, Aunt Hattie and my mom wistfully recall the fish they sold as young girls. "Do you ever get butterfish in?"

they ask me. "It was delicious." Butterfish do still exist, but they're too small to smoke; nowadays, they are mostly used as bait. At its best, butterfish was sweet and looked like a round-bellied chub. You had to be careful when eating it because of its many small bones, and you would want to avoid the black, bitter meat on the bottom of the fish. But the butterfish-eating crowd was adept at avoiding the bad parts and feasting on the sweetness of the major portion of this fish. Today, people don't like to deal with fish bones, so this one fell out of favor and is no longer sold.

Russian White Lox: By the time I took over the business in 1978, Russian white lox (beloribitsa) was no longer sold in the store; it had been overfished and was unavailable. But I do remember it as a kid. A type of salmon that was native to the Caspian Sea, it was actually earthy beige in color rather than pure white. Its distinguishing feature was its fattiness, which made it a treat for all real fish lovers who understand that when it comes to fish, the fatter it is, the better it is. In those days, the salmon would be sliced and the slices laid out on sheets of wet wax paper. The beloribitsa was so fatty that the slices often slid off the paper, sometimes to the floor.

When people come into the store looking for beluga caviar, butterfish, or beloribitsa, they're often looking to recapture a taste experience from their own food memory or from that of an aging parent or grandparent. We give them the bad news with a lengthy explanation of why we no longer carry these items—they were fished out, or they're too salty or too bony for today's tastes. But no one asks for kapchunka anymore.

Kapchunka: When Is a Fish Not a Fish?

When Grandpa Russ renovated the store in 1950, he hand-stenciled the names of the various products we sold—Nova Scotia, lake sturgeon, whitefish, herring, pickles, olives, et cetera—in big black letters along the soffit above the top shelves. This architectural feature still exists today at Russ & Daughters.

The section of the soffit that is visible through the front window, the first one seen by passersby in the street, reads SMOKED EEL. Smoked eel, a non-kosher fish, was sold in the store only during the Christmas holidays to non-Jewish Eastern European customers. Eel was never displayed in the showcase. Jews didn't eat smoked eels, nor did they like looking at them. Compared to the other fish in the showcase, eel is ugly and snakelike in appearance, and so it was kept in the refrigerator in the back of the store. I once asked my mother and Aunt Hattie why Grandpa Russ promoted this *trayfe* item so prominently on our walls. It had never even occurred to them to ask him. "That's what Papa wanted, and that was that," they replied. *Shoyn. Fartig.* Case closed.

The next soffit section reads KAPCHUNKA. Customers often ask, "What's a kapchunka?" Kapchunka is a salted and air-dried whitefish with its guts still inside. We sold kapchunka in the store until about twenty years ago. To air-dry the fish we would place twine through the mouth and gills and then hang the fish from hooks in the front of the store. As the fat dripped out, the fish would get drier, saltier, and chewier. A special treat for the kapchunka eater was to find roe when they cut open the belly of the fish. Alas, the enjoyment of kapchunka wasn't passed from generation to generation. I wonder why.

Because kapchunkas aren't refrigerated and are dried with the guts intact, they can be dangerous if not processed correctly by producers or handled properly by retailers. In 1985 an elderly Russian American couple died of botulism poisoning from consuming kapchunka purchased at a Queens appetizing store. The Food and Drug Administration immediately sent out an all-points bulletin to the appetizing world in search of the deadly fish and issued a nationwide Class I recall. By that time, we had so few customers who ate kapchunka that we were no longer carrying it. Nowadays, for those customers who see the name on the soffit and ask about it, I'm happy to explain what it is.

There's one other family story about kapchunka. Some time ago my second cousin Steven Ebbin came across an old, yellowing, undated newspaper clipping with the heading "When Is a Fish Not a Fish?" It told the story of Channah Russ Ebbin, Steven's grandmother, and sister and mentor to Grandpa Russ, who had received a summons for violating a new law that required fish sold to the public to be kept under refrigeration. According to the article, Channah Ebbin, acting as her own lawyer, presented a novel defense: this was not fish that she was selling; it was "kapchunka." She explained to the judge that kapchunka did not require refrigeration, and that in fact refrigerating them would ruin their taste. Nobody would buy a cold kapchunka, she testified. She won the case.

The Candy Side: A Little Something Sweet

Men and women of Grandpa Russ's generation always kept individually wrapped hard candies in their pockets or purses, because you never knew when you might have a coughing fit or encounter a child who needed a treat. Grandpa Russ had his favorites: hopjes, coffee-flavored cubes made in Holland; Napoleon Lemon Sours, which became more tart as you sucked them; Israeli fruit-filled, with pretty pictures of fruit on the wrapper and a chewy, fruity center; English Crystal Mints, a definite breath aid; and sesame honey candies that were often quite sticky after being carried around in his pocket all day, especially in the summertime. Grandpa enjoyed dispensing these candies to his grandchildren, a small act of sweetness from a man not given to displays of affection. Those of us who didn't run away when he tried to scare us by removing his false teeth were rewarded with a candy.

It's not known when appetizing stores began selling confections as a counterpoint to the salty, smoky, and pickled flavors of the fish and herring, but the model eventually became the standard. When Grandpa Russ enlarged and renovated the store in 1950, a separate area was devoted to the sucking candies he and his contemporaries favored, and to dried fruits that were used in compotes (assorted fruit slowly cooked in a sugar syrup and often served as dessert). The entire window of the candy side of the store was lined with overflowing bins of dried fruits: apricots, pears, peaches, apples, and two different kinds of prunes—jumbo prunes from California and sour prunes from Oregon. Hanging just above the dried fruits were strings of dried Polish mushrooms, which were then plentiful and cheap. (Today they sell for $200 a pound!) These deeply flavored, earthy mushrooms were often used as a meat substitute in thick, hearty barley soups during difficult economic times, when meat was just too expensive for some people.

By the time I started working in the store on weekends in 1958, just after my bar mitzvah, there were many new additions to the candy side: candied ginger, caramels, pineapple cores, apricots, prunes, and orange peels, all hand-dipped in chocolate. Little chocolate balls filled with rum flavoring. A mixture of chocolate-covered candied fruit and nuts called bridge mix. Sheets of dark chocolate with whole roasted almonds partially buried within, called almond bark. Chocolate-covered marshmallows called twists, which customers stored in their freezers and ate frozen. Imported pistachios from Iran, figs from Turkey, dates from Syria, sugar-glazed fruit from Australia. Chocolate-covered jelly rings, jelly bars, and halvah (in chocolate, vanilla, marble, and marble-with-nuts varieties). The newly created candy side was run in the same manner as the fish side: buy the best products available in the marketplace, handle them carefully, and make sure there's a Russ around to sell them.

Since there's little demand today for individually wrapped hard candies, I relegated them to a few jars on a bottom shelf when I renovated the store in 1995. Gummy candies are the preferred sweet of today's youngsters. When kids begin to show signs of impatience while their parents are buying fish, I offer them a choice of a complimentary gummy worm, gummy fish, or gummy bear. Studying the jars and deciding which animal to select takes serious thought. Then it takes time to choose the color—red, yellow, green, or orange. The kids are occupied, the parents are relieved, and the Russ tradition of dispensing candies is maintained.

Nowadays, customers come in looking for the sweets they haven't had since they were kids or have heard about only from their parents or grandparents: chocolate-covered halvah squares; marshmallow-wrapped apricots and prunes; orange-and-red-layered marmalade bars covered with chocolate sprinkles; candied kumquats in heavy, sticky syrup; and Indian nuts. While these items no longer exist, we have many other sweets to choose from to make our customers happy: babka, rugelach, hand-dipped chocolates and truffles, mountains of halvah. And the display in the window is still filled with overflowing bins of dried fruits—which are still ideal for fruit compotes.

So, What's New?

When Niki and Josh were fairly new to running the store, Maria and I decided to take a two-week vacation. We left with our normal vacation angst: Would the store still be there when we returned? To our relief, Russ & Daughters was, in fact, in one piece when we got back. Then I overheard a customer step up to the counter and ask for a "Super Heeb."

"What the hell is that about?" I asked Josh. He pointed to the sandwich menu, which now had in bold letters: "NEW ITEM: THE SUPER HEEB. Sesame bagel, horseradish cream cheese, whitefish salad, and wasabi-flavored flying fish roe."

As I had feared, the store was about to go under.

"Josh, you can't do this!" I said.

"Why not?"

"Why not? Are you kidding? This is offensive on every level! I realize that my sister raised you on an ashram and you lived on the West Coast, but in this town there are two words you cannot use: one begins with an *N* and the other with an *H.* The *N* you obviously know. The *H* stands for 'Heeb,' and it doesn't make it any more acceptable to put a 'super' in front of it. Yes, one Jew might be able to call another a Heeb in private, as an inside joke, with no one else around. But that's it. I'm chalking this mistake up to your out-of-the-city communal upbringing."

My restraint masked my anger, and in my anger I felt a channeling of the outrage of the previous generations of Russes who had run this as a traditional ethnic store, selling mostly Jewish food to mostly Jewish customers in what was once a mostly Jewish neighborhood, where the only people who called you "Heeb" in public were the ones who were about to beat you up because you were a Jew.

Josh offered something of an explanation: "It's delicious. People love it. Let me make you one to try."

"No way!" I replied. "Josh, you don't get it. It's not just ethnically offensive in its name, it's also gastronomically offensive. You can't stick all of this weird stuff together in one sandwich—especially in this store. In our little corner of the world, we are the traditional appetizing store. A bagel with cream cheese and lox is the traditional sandwich. If you want to add a slice of tomato or onion to that combination, well, that's about as crazy as you can get with this food."

Josh listened quietly, nodded in apparent agreement, and then, as usual, ignored me.

While I considered whether to draw a line in the cream cheese and demand that Josh and Niki rename the sandwich, or perhaps reconsider their futures as smoked-fish-mongers, an issue of *Time Out New York* magazine appeared with a full-page photo of Russ & Daughters' new Super Heeb sandwich. The magazine identified it as one of the great taste sensations in New York and named it an "Editor's Pick." I watched in disbelief as customers lined up to buy Super Heebs.

Among those who saw the *Time Out* article were Jeremy and Lisa, a couple from Boston. They had never visited the Lower East Side and decided to come for a weekend and sample the now-famous Super Heeb sandwich. They fell so in love with the sandwich, with Russ & Daughters, and with the Lower East Side that they decided to relocate to the neighborhood. They moved into a newly constructed luxury condominium on the corner of East Houston and Ludlow, one block from the store. The building has a concierge and a health club. (That location used to be the parking lot where we kept the store van. Nowadays, the Lower East Side is so full of trendy buildings, we have to park in a lot that's ten blocks away.) One day, Jeremy came in without Lisa. He ordered a Super Heeb and placed a diamond ring in the package. When he proposed, Lisa said yes.

My sense of outrage eventually changed to a sense of pride as the new generation began to make its mark: new products, new customers. In the Russ family, business trumps tradition. Josh and Niki ultimately agreed to a compromise. Their new, wildly successful creation is now known as the "Super Heebster."

In spite of my going on and on about our food traditions and our ancestors rolling over in their graves, I, too, introduced new products over the years. These new items were added to accommodate changes in taste, because certain time-honored products were no longer available, and because I also understood that we had to keep things interesting for our customers.

Early on in my smoked-fish career, it became clear that the younger generation of smoked-fish eaters didn't want bones in their fish. If they could, they would genetically engineer boneless fish. Smoked salmon, sturgeon, and sable were no problem, because they were sliced from fillets. But whitefish and chub sales were trending downward. The art of peeling the moist fish flesh away from the bone died with their parents' and grandparents' generations. The current generation seemed to be terrified of dying from—or at least choking on—fish bones. Which was why turning whitefish meat into a salad or spread was an immediate hit with all generations.

Figuring out what to do with the dark part of the salmon, closest to the skin, was more difficult. Old-timers know that this is a rich, tasty layer of fish fat and would object if it was trimmed away. "What are you doing?" they would shout at me. "You're losing the best part of the fish. Cut down to the skin." We rarely hear that anymore. Now it's a shriek if there is a speck of dark in an otherwise salmon-colored slice. No use in trying to convince customers that this part of the fish is delicious. So we came up with Smoked Salmon Tartare—a delectable solution. (See recipe on page 158.) The fact that we use smoked salmon and not raw salmon should be chalked up to culinary poetic license.

We also devised a creative solution to the problem of what to do with bagels left over at the end of the day. Day-old bagels are not sold at our store. Offering a "baker's dozen" sold some; "half price for the last hour" sold a few more. But we still had a considerable amount of leftovers. When the neighborhood streets were populated by Bowery bums and prostitutes, I handed them out to the locals, but I had to abandon that when the crowd got large and unruly and some demanded cream cheese and lox on their free bagels. Then we hit upon Bagel Pudding, which is very much like a bread pudding and has become very popular on the newly hip Lower East Side. (See recipe on page 191.)

Perhaps my greatest assault on a classic food tradition was the creation of a new gefilte fish preparation. While there have always been variations on the gefilte fish theme, most traditional recipes include whitefish, pike, and mullet. Some prefer their gefilte fish sweet, others savory. Some like fish shaped into ovals; others want loaves. But in either case, gefilte fish sales were trending down. Our new salmon, whitefish, and dill creation has more in common with French quenelles than with traditional gefilte fish, and it can be served hot or cold as an appetizer at the fanciest dinner party. It brought our sales back up, and so gefilte fish survives for another generation.

It's important to give credit where it's due: The creation of these new products was my idea, but the development of the recipes has been the work of my wife, Maria, who is not a Russ by birth and, God bless her, is not afraid of breaking with tradition.

Maria, my partner in life and in work, and me at our daughter Niki's wedding in 2007

Whitefish and Baked Salmon Salad

MAKES 8 SERVINGS

1½ pounds smoked whitefish, skinned and boned (about one 2-pound whitefish)
½ pound kippered (hot smoked) salmon
¾ cup mayonnaise
½ small white onion, finely minced
¼ teaspoon white pepper

With your fingers, flake the whitefish and salmon, making sure to remove any skin and bones. Transfer the fish to a food processor and pulse until it is well combined yet still slightly chunky, about 5 or 6 one-second pulses. Transfer the fish to a large bowl and gently fold in the mayonnaise, onion, and white pepper with a spatula.

Smoked Salmon Tartare

MAKES 24 SERVINGS

2½ pounds smoked salmon (preferably a mild variety, such as Gaspé Atlantic or Western Nova)
1 medium red onion, finely diced
½ cup finely chopped scallions (white and light green parts only)
2 tablespoons red wine vinegar
1½ teaspoons extra virgin olive oil
1 tablespoon minced fresh parsley

Cut the smoked salmon into a ¼-inch dice. Combine the salmon, red onion, scallions, vinegar, olive oil, and parsley in a large bowl and mix gently until just blended. Serve with endive leaves, crackers, or bagel chips.

7

The Holidays

All Year Round

Back when I was a trial lawyer working at a prestigious Manhattan law firm, my parents were certainly proud of the fact that I was the first professional in the family. But when the Jewish holidays arrived in September or October, it didn't matter how many degrees or how many pending cases I had, they expected me to leave my clients for a few days and help them out behind the counter. In fact, I occasionally had to ask a judge for a delay in a trial. If the judge was Jewish, he understood. And often the judge would ask me to put in his holiday order when I got to the store.

Home for the Holidays

Once I took over at Russ & Daughters, I would call my kids each autumn as the Jewish holidays approached to ask them to help *me* out. When they got cell phones with the ability to screen and avoid calls, it often took several attempts to reach them, because they knew why I was calling. But I was not about to be deterred. We are the Russ family. When you're needed, you come home for the holidays.

One year, Noah protested that his professors at Mount Sinai School of Medicine wouldn't accept any excuses for missing classes. "Dad, I can't tell my prof that I have to miss a week of neurosurgery classes to slice salmon."

"*Vi nempt men parnosa?*" I replied, using Grandpa Russ's family mantra. "From where do we make our living? How do we survive?" I also reminded him—in English—that I, meaning the store, had been paying for his education. Noah showed up on time and ready for work. As it turned out, some of his professors were not only understanding about his absence from school but also asked him to fill their holiday orders. One of his classmates even volunteered to help out in the store in exchange for smoked fish to take home to his family for the holidays. I assigned Noah and his friend to packing orders. They were the fastest and most accurate order-packing team we ever had. Finally, his expensive education was paying off.

Then there was the time that I called Niki while she was studying abroad and said I needed her in the store.

"Dad, don't you remember?" she said. "I'm in France. I can't make it for the holidays this year."

"Really? What are you doing there?" I was teasing; of course I knew very well that our herring sales were paying for her tuition at L'Institut d'Études Politiques de Paris. And, come to think of it, the store had paid for her French lessons as well. I told Niki that geography wasn't a problem. I'd pay for the round-trip ticket, and she could study on the plane to New York and on the plane going back to Paris. She came home and brought along a French-Vietnamese friend who was curious about American culture. Her friend didn't speak much English, and our customers rarely speak French or Vietnamese, so I assigned her to packing bagels. All went well until a customer asked her for "assorted" bagels. We had taught her only about "mixed" bagels. But we worked it out. And a week later Niki and her friend—who must have picked up some interesting ideas about American culture from working at Russ & Daughters for ten hours a day—were back on the plane to Paris.

This is how it is in a family business. The small family-owned-and-operated store is not unlike the small family farm. You gather everyone for the harvest season and they all pitch in. And you never know if the harvest will be bountiful or if an act of nature or of inhumanity will ruin all of your hard work.

The New Year and September 11, 2001

I am cursing as I walk down First Avenue from Fourteenth Street. I'm on my way back to the store with Raul, the kitchen man, each of us pushing a hand truck containing ten boxes filled with assorted smoked fish. Everyone's used to my cursing in the store (but not when there are customers around, of course), so Raul isn't taking it personally; he isn't even paying attention. It's September 13, 2001, two days after the terrorist attacks on the World Trade Center in downtown Manhattan, and all vehicular traffic has been banned south of Fourteenth Street, which has been cordoned off. To get products to the store for the upcoming Jewish holidays, we have to walk fourteen blocks north to Fourteenth Street, meet the delivery trucks coming from the smokehouses, and then schlep the boxes fourteen blocks back to Houston Street.

The period from Rosh Hashanah to Yom Kippur is Russ & Daughters' busiest time of the year, and Rosh Hashanah is just days away. But with traffic banned in the neighborhood and mass transit service spotty at best, how will our customers get to the store? And will shoppers want to come down to Lower Manhattan after the ban is lifted? It's clear to me that this event will have a devastating economic impact on New York City, and especially on Lower Manhattan. And there is no way to know how long it will last.

On the morning of September 11, 2001, Herman and I were working behind the counter and Niki was in the upstairs office when I got a call from Maria. It was about 9:15. Maria had heard on the radio and then seen on TV that something terrible had happened at the World Trade Center. Apparently a plane had crashed into the North Tower, and the building was on fire. Maria suggested that we go up to the roof of our building, where we would have a clear and unobstructed view of the World Trade Center, less than a mile away. Then Maria called again, telling us that a second plane had crashed into the South Tower and that it might be a terrorist attack. Niki, Herman, and I went up to the roof. The skies were the kind of bright, clear blue that you see in New York only a couple of times a year. We stood there, speechless, watching the two towers burning. It wasn't long before they collapsed. Herman, who tends to have an apocalyptic view of things, was convinced that this was the end of the world. Given what we had just witnessed, I thought it was possible that he was right this time.

We went back downstairs, and I went over to the corner of East Houston and Allen. Walking past me, going north, were hundreds of people, some covered with soot and ash, all looking bewildered. Some asked if they could use our bathroom or our phone. (Our bathroom was working, but not the phones.) Some just needed to talk. No one had much information about what had just happened or what was going to happen. There was a communal state of shock.

Once we determined that no one who worked in the store had loved ones in or near the World Trade Center that day, I sent home employees who would have difficulty traveling or who needed to gather their families. I closed the store at 3:00 p.m., and Niki and I rode our bicycles to the World Trade Center site. We knew without discussing it that this was a historic, unprecedented event. Traveling by bike was easy. All vehicular traffic had been halted except for ambulances, fire trucks, and police cars, all with sirens screaming at the same time. No one paid any attention to two people on bikes. We got as far as about three blocks from what has since become known as Ground Zero. Many of the streets in this part of Manhattan are narrow and lined with tall buildings, making them feel almost like caverns. Those caverns were now acting as funnels for white smoke and gray ash. Every few minutes a firefighter emerged from the smoke cloud, alone and exhausted, where we stood with our bikes. When it became clear that there was nothing we could do to help, Niki bicycled back home to her apartment over the store, and I bicycled over the Brooklyn Bridge to our home in Brooklyn, accompanied by hundreds of bewildered-looking people who were walking across the bridge to get home as well. None of us could yet fathom the depth of this tragedy.

Many of the neighborhood businesses closed down for the duration, but on September 12 I made the decision to keep Russ & Daughters open every day, for full ten-hour days. We represented something enduring and reliable in a changing neighborhood during changing times. A sense of stability and normalcy was needed for our employees, our customers, and me, now that our world had been turned upside down. And nothing was going to stop the Jewish holidays from arriving a week later.

Rosh Hashanah that year fell on September 18. I expected very little business in the days leading up to the holiday. Traffic into Manhattan was restricted, and subway service was only gradually coming back. But some people—not many—did come. Some used the subways and some walked, schlepping home shopping bags filled with smoked fish. Business was way off, as it was for everyone in the neighborhood.

Ten days after Rosh Hashanah comes Yom Kippur, the Day of Atonement, the holiest day on the Jewish calendar. Jews observe a twenty-five-hour fast from sundown to sundown, which is traditionally followed by a celebratory "break-fast" meal that is shared with family and friends. Providing food for this meal makes this period the busiest time of the year for Russ & Daughters. But that year, I expected the worst. As Yom Kippur drew closer, traveling around Manhattan became a bit easier. Some customers canceled their long-standing orders, but others increased the size of theirs because they were inviting more people to their break-fast. Some told me that they had lost family members or friends to this tragedy and didn't feel like celebrating anything, but they felt that they wanted to, they needed to, maintain the tradition of the Yom Kippur break-fast with food from Russ & Daughters. That made me feel a bit better, but not much.

Breakfast? No, It's Break-Fast

Older customers who came from Eastern Europe told me that the traditional Yom Kippur break-fast used to be nothing more than a piece of schmaltz herring and a shot of schnapps. The herring quickly put some salt into the fasting body, and the schnapps was for . . . everything else. Pulling a herring or two or three from the barrel—the cost was three for a quarter in the early 1920s—and wrapping it in a Yiddish newspaper didn't take very long. There were no pre-orders, no lines, no waiting.

Yom Kippur is a day of repentance and fasting as atonement for the previous year's accumulated sins. During this twenty-five-hour period, any work—including cooking—is forbidden. So over the years, and with the increasing affluence of American Jews, the break-fast food of choice expanded from herring to other food that didn't require cooking or even reheating once the services were over: smoked and cured fish; bagels and bialys with a schmear of cream cheese; and rugelach and babka for dessert.

What this means for Russ & Daughters is that hordes of Jews descend on our store during the week leading up to Yom Kippur. Five thousand years of poverty, privation, and pogroms have programmed into our DNA a primal fear that any fast at any time could become permanent. Matters are further complicated by the fact that our fish, although smoked, pickled, and cured, is still perishable, with a shelf life of one week to ten days. Add to this the fact that some of our products are not plentiful and may indeed run out before the onset of the holidays. The result: hundreds of pre-fasting Jews who think they may never eat again shopping at the last minute and waiting in line for products that may run out before it's their turn to be waited on. The chaos that this creates is probably not hard to visualize.

When I ran the store, I did everything during the pre-holiday rush. I sliced, diced, and filleted fish and kept the counter clean—always a knife in my hand, always a rag in my pocket. I answered the phones and the customers' questions, kept the countermen energized, and maintained crowd control as best I could.

It was not unusual in the midst of all the craziness to get a phone call from an elderly woman who was hard-of-hearing. The conversation usually went something like this:

"Are you the boss?"

"Yes, I'm Mr. Russ."

"I want a quarter pound of lox, you should slice it thin, and two bagels, they should be well baked but not burnt. I'm sending my son to pick it up in half an hour. Make sure it's ready."

"I'm sorry. We're too busy. It's the holidays. I'm afraid I can't take your order over the phone."

"What?"

"I can't take your order."

"I don't have a daughter. I said I'm sending my son."

"No, I said I can't take your order."

"That's right, a quarter."

I see this is no use. It takes longer to communicate than to simply fill the order.

"Okay, okay. It's the holidays, so why don't you buy a half a pound?"

For some reason, she hears this clearly. "A half a pound? What am I making? A wedding?"

Even though I'm now retired, I'm still called into service by Niki and Josh for the pre-holiday rush. But now I stand on the customers' side of the counter, wearing civilian clothes, not the deli whites—the long white starched coat with the Russ & Daughters fish logo over the breast pocket. And now I get to smile as I walk through the shop, helping to control the chaos.

It wasn't always such a pleasure. For my parents, aunts, uncles, and grandparents it was *a lebn* (a living), and not an easy one: Jewish merchants selling Jewish food to Jewish customers in a Jewish ghetto, with plenty of competition from other appetizing stores and a clientele barely out of poverty themselves. How much things have changed. These days, during the Jewish holiday season the shop is packed to capacity, with many people waiting outside to get in and customers who have made it into the store waiting their turn to step up to the counter and select the smoked fish, herring, salads, and other items they will have sliced, diced, filleted, and packaged to take home for their own break-fast. There are five employees handing out the pre-placed orders, ten working the fish counter, three on the candy side, two in the basement shipping area, six in the kitchen, and one (me) attempting some sort of crowd control.

On the days leading up to Yom Kippur, the wait for service ranges from two to three hours. Often a customer will approach me and ask how long I think the wait will be. She holds number 27 and the above-the-counter monitor shows that customer number 15 is currently being waited on. "About two hours," I reply. She can't understand. "How can it take two hours to wait on twelve customers?" I explain that she has number C27 and they are now taking care of number B15. There are more than one hundred numbers in between.

On one particular day–before–Yom Kippur a few years ago, the customers outside the store aren't unhappy at all; in fact, the mood is festive even though they're about to begin a twenty-five-hour fast and a period of deep introspection and atonement. The weather is nice, an atypically sunny and mild day in the beginning of October. This time of year it's often cold and rainy, and the customers outside are as unhappy about waiting in the rain as they are about their impending deprivation. But now, in addition to the nice weather, they are also being entertained. Niki hired a klezmer band to play for two hours

The schmoozer in chief with Niki and Josh, the fourth-generation owners of Russ & Daughters. Grandpa Russ is kvelling.
(Copyright © Belathée Photography)

outside the store. When I first heard about this, I was shocked. This had never been done before! It was not part of the traditional pre–Yom Kippur scene at Russ & Daughters, and it could be regarded only as insensitive to the gravity of the occasion. But, as usual, I am proved wrong. The customers are happy to be diverted by the klezmer music, which is culturally in sync with the foods they are about to buy: here are both the food and the music of their Jewish souls. They are even buying the band's CDs.

There is, however, the perennial problem of those customers who took a number, waited for a while, then got hungry and went down the block to Katz's for a hot dog or a pastrami sandwich, or walked three blocks to put more money in the meter. They missed their number when it was called and they look to me for dispensation. This always creates a dilemma in my mind: Who is the customer? Where did he go? Is she one of our regulars? Will taking them out of turn because they missed their number cause a riot? I usually just say, "I'm sorry, you need to take a new number." No *rachmonis* (sympathy), not even on *erev* Yom Kippur.

This time I am approached by one of our regulars. Roy is a jazz musician, a longtime but now former resident of the Lower East Side. Roy was once part of the local artists/writers/musicians scene, but he felt compelled to move to Brooklyn when he got married and had a child. He misses the old neighborhood and is not very comfortable with the new, trendy Lower East Side. Roy also found it necessary to get a steady day job, teaching music at a Brooklyn school. He tells me that his next class is in one hour and I *have* to bump him up in the line. I tell him I'm sorry but I can't, and he paces back and forth nervously. Here is a serious moral dilemma. Roy decides that it is better for the teacher to cut his class than to miss his number at Russ & Daughters.

Don't Hand Me a Line. Get on It.

I have to admit it, our customers are a creative bunch. Especially when it comes to devising excuses for jumping the line during the holidays. I've heard everything. Many require me to exercise the wisdom of a Solomon to resolve, but since I'm no Solomon, I usually just say no. I've been offered everything from money to—well, use your imagination. The bottom line is: If you come to Russ & Daughters to shop before a major holiday, be prepared to wait in line. Here are some of my favorite excuses offered up by people who just don't want to:

1. *My mother just died.* It was true, but what does that have to do with buying herring?
2. *I have a patient waiting on the operating table.* A favorite of many doctors past and present. Nice try, but it doesn't work.
3. *I was in Europe all summer. You can't expect me to put in my order from overseas?* Why not? We have a customer who places his Yom Kippur order every year from wherever he is on his travels. One year he called me from the Great Wall in China.
4. *I was in the Hamptons all summer.* See number 3.

5. *I was at the hospital with my daughter, who broke her leg.* Okay, I let him jump the line because he showed up in the store with his daughter in a cast and a wheelchair.

Sometimes mothers or fathers bring their young children to the store and get them to scream on command, expecting that I will immediately want the family waited on to get them out of the store. Instead, I offer the child a piece of candy, which calms down the kid but agitates the parent.

Some regular customers, unhappy that they must wait their turn with the "once-a-year types," suggest, as directly and abruptly as pre-fasting Jews can, that I "put on a white coat, get behind the counter, and move the line faster." Or, short of that, just "cut me a pound of lox and give me some herring fillets in cream sauce so I don't have to stand on my feet." I politely refuse. They can't believe it. They're not used to seeing me on their side of the counter. They are confused.

"What are you doing over here?" they ask.

"I'm retired," I say. They don't believe me.

"What are you gonna do in retirement?"

"I'm gonna write a book about this place," I reply.

There is another line within the store before the holidays. This line leads from the retail space in front to the prep area at the rear of the store, an area usually restricted to employees. But on these pre-holiday days the line overflows into the kitchen and consists of people waiting to pick up orders they placed in advance by telephone. Since Russ & Daughters sells mostly perishable products, we can take only a certain number of advance orders. It is well known throughout New York and its greater metropolitan area that those who have made it onto the Russ & Daughters Yom Kippur Order List have achieved a certain status. While this symbol of success is not assignable, it is inheritable. If your grandmother was on the list but is no longer alive or capable of ordering and the mantle of "keeping the holidays" has been passed to you, you get on the list. You do not get on the list if you are a Russ relative or a personal friend. Not even if you used to play pinochle with my father and uncles.

The people on the order pickup line wait about half an hour—not the two hours it would take to get waited on with a number at the counter—but it shouldn't even take this long. The slowness of this line directly relates to what the Jews of the greater New York area feel is the basic problem with ordering takeout, which is the assumption that there will always be something missing from your order.

"Show me where you put the two pounds of sable" is a common refrain. This may require unpacking and repacking several cartons filled with merchandise. Or, if nothing is missing, there is, on reflection, "not enough." Our religion has eleven commandments, and the eleventh is: "Thou shalt not run out of food." A typical dialogue goes as follows:

"I have seven people coming for the break-fast. How much lox do I need?"

"One pound."

"How much lox did I order?"

"Three pounds."

"Good. Cut me another quarter of a pound."

Since it's mostly the same people waiting on line every year, they often take the opportunity to catch up on the previous year's events.

"Did your son finish law school?"

"Is your daughter still married to the orthopedic surgeon? I have a terrible pain in my hip [or knee, or shoulder]."

"Did your husband have his prostate operation?"

"Did your granddaughter get into Dalton [or Harvard, or Yale]?"

I have observed two politicians working out some piece of legislation as they waited on line. And I wish I had a buck for every business transaction that was consummated while our customers waited to be served. Lots of business cards are exchanged, and sometimes even telephone numbers. Who knows how many marriages can be chalked up to the pre–Yom Kippur line at Russ & Daughters?

On one occasion a well-known New York theatrical producer and regular customer came to pick up his order. It was checked and handed to him by Noah, who was on temporary forced leave from medical school to work the pre-holiday rush. The producer emerged from the back of the store with his carton and came over to me.

"Mark," he said, "we have to do something about this."

"Something about what?"

"Your son and my daughter. I just spent time with Noah, and he would be perfect for my daughter."

I didn't know whether this was because Noah was going to be a doctor or because our family was in the food business.

"She's a pastry chef at Bouley," he said.

Now I knew. "Listen," I replied. "I learned the hard way to stay out of my kids' lives, especially their social lives."

"We're two Jewish fathers. This is what we're supposed to do."

"Sorry, I'm out of this one."

Undaunted, the producer put down his order and returned to the back of the store. He emerged within minutes with a big smile.

"I did it," he said.

"What did you do?"

"I got your son's telephone number." I had no idea why he thought this was a victory until late that night after work, when I got a call from Noah.

"Dad, what should I do?"

"About what?"

"There is a message on my answering machine from that producer. He left his daughter's telephone number and said that I should call her."

"Well, Noah, it's entirely up to you. He's a very nice guy and a good customer. Someday I may need him for house seats to some show, but I will not get involved in this. Look at it this way: Remember the chocolate soufflé at Bouley that you love? Well, he says that his daughter is a pastry chef there. Even if this doesn't work out, you can come away with the recipe."

They went out. It didn't work. And Noah didn't even get the recipe. He also never went out with a customer's daughter after that—though many tried.

We Pray at the Store

We're not a religious family—never have been since Grandpa Russ came to America. In the Old Country, the Russes followed the teachings and dictates of Hasidic Judaism. But Grandpa Russ felt that religion had not served him, his family, or his people particularly well, and to him this new land meant a new life unencumbered by its strictures. He wasn't deliberately irreligious or anti-religious; he just didn't have time for religion. He was too busy simply trying to survive, and he refused to submit his business to the constraints and limitations of religion. He kept his store open on Shabbos (for which Grandma Russ branded him a *shtick goy,* a Jew who ignores his religion) because many Jews living on the Lower East Side were secular and bought smoked fish, bagels, and cream cheese on Saturdays to eat on Sunday mornings with their families. And he did not want to restrict himself to selling only kosher varieties of fish. On the other hand, he always went to shul during the High Holy Days and could recite all of the prayers in perfect Hebrew—one of the few feats in his repertoire that did impress his daughters.

Nowadays, all Russ family members happily identify ourselves as cultural Jews, and we do little bits here and there to keep that sense of identity alive. My wife and I attend services at the Reform temple in our Brooklyn neighborhood, where we have been longtime members.

Each year I looked forward to attending the service on the eve of Yom Kippur, just to hear the Kol Nidrei prayer. Ever since I first heard it as a child in synagogue, it has always had special meaning for me. When it's properly sung or performed, this beautiful prayer gives me a spiritual connection, a sense of transcendence about Judaism. My favorite version, a composition for cello and orchestra, was written by Max Bruch, a nineteenth-century gentile composer. For years I searched for someone who could play Bruch's version the way I first heard it as a kid.

One Saturday morning shortly after Yom Kippur, I arrived to find the store buzzing with activity—lots of customers being served and waiting to be served. I stood in front of the counter, schmoozing, and noticed a young man in his thirties carrying a cello case and looking around. It was clearly his first time in the store. I asked him if he could play the cello.

"I'm only minding it for someone else," he responded.

"Too bad. I would have traded you a sandwich for a song," I said.

He quickly changed his mind. "I can play," he said.

"But can you play Kol Nidrei?"

He had an Australian accent and didn't look Jewish, so I figured I'd call his bluff and avoid a free sandwich.

"How does it go?" he asked. I hummed a few bars from memory.

"Oh," he said. "That's the Max Bruch piece. I haven't played it since I was ten years old, but I can give it a try if you have a chair."

He seemed determined to get that free sandwich. A chair was brought from the back, and he readied himself as the regular noises of commerce continued, oblivious to a musician with a cello seated alongside the herring showcase. But once he started to play, all the background noise stopped immediately; in fact, all business stopped. Everyone—countermen, kitchen men, and customers—was focused on the cellist. His notes were clear, precise, rich, and deep. The melody was true. There wasn't a dry eye in the store. My own heart stopped, and my eyes filled with tears. I was there, but I also felt as though I'd been transported somewhere else. It was a transcendent experience. When he finished there was great applause, and then, without a moment's transition, the noise of commerce resumed:

"Give me a chub from underneath; it should be a nice one."

"I need extra onions with my herring."

I stepped behind the counter and personally made the cellist my own favorite sandwich: a thin schmear of cream cheese on a bagel, heaps of Scottish salmon, a slice of sturgeon, and a slice of tomato. He and I acknowledged that this had been a very New York, very Russ & Daughters moment that could never be repeated, anywhere.

Some months later Niki was at a party where she was introduced to a woman who said she was a longtime customer of the store. When told that Niki was a member of the Russ family, the woman smiled and said, "I was at Russ & Daughters on that Saturday back in October, for Kol Nidrei."

The Great Jewish Divide

Two days before Rosh Hashanah in 2010 I was standing in front of the counter, holding court in the middle of the holiday crowd and providing some entertainment for the waiting customers. I had just begun my regular *shpiel* ("My grandfather, Joel Russ, came to this country, to the Lower East Side, in 1907 and sold herrings from a pushcart on—") when I heard a woman's voice from somewhere in the crowd.

"*My* family came to this country in 1654," she said.

I looked up to see a woman who appeared to be somewhere between sixty and seventy years old (I later found out that she was eighty), sporting a bicycle helmet.

"Jewish?" I asked.

"Yes."

"Sephardic?" I guessed.

"Yes."

This lady's story would be more interesting than mine, so I made my way through the crowd to her. Everyone gathered around both of us.

"Have you been here before?" I asked.

"Oh, my, yes. I've been coming here since I was a young girl."

I did not expect to hear this from a Sephardic Jew, and I asked if she'd share her family's story. As it turned out, she was a direct descendant of Jews who were advisers in the court of the king of Spain, but who were expelled from Spain in 1492 and from Portugal in 1497 when they refused to convert to Catholicism. They traveled to Holland, which was known for its religious tolerance, but found the weather too cold and the language too difficult, and so they immigrated to the formerly Portuguese colony of Recife, Brazil, where both the weather and the language were more in sync with their Iberian roots. But the Inquisition followed them to Recife, when what had become a Dutch colony was reconquered by the Portuguese in 1654. So her family fled once again, intending to return to Holland. The next part of the story had something to do with pirates on the high seas, and her family, part of a group of twenty-three Recife Jews, found themselves heading for New Amsterdam, as New York was then called, back when it was a Dutch colony. There was some initial hope of religious freedom and a good life in this new land, but the Dutch governor, Peter Stuyvesant, turned out to be an anti-Semite and refused to allow the Recife Jews to settle permanently in Manhattan. (It's pretty ironic that so many Jews now live in a famous housing development on Manhattan's East Side that bears his name.) This necessitated the intervention of the Dutch West

India Company, which had Jews on its board of directors, and since the board was paying Stuyvesant's salary, he saw the light and let the Recife Jews stay. These Sephardim then set up businesses; established the first synagogue in America, Shearith Israel; and became members of New York's elite, fully involved in the public life of colonial America.

The Sephardim I was used to seeing in the store were Jews who came to America in the 1950s and '60s, when they were expelled from Muslim countries in North Africa and the Middle East. Our smoked-fish products, traditional Ashkenazi fare, were not what they had been raised on, and it took them a generation or two to develop a taste for them. As far as I knew, this woman was unique in being a descendant of New York's seventeenth-century Sephardic community who was also a regular Russ & Daughters customer. When she finished relating her family's history, I asked her how her family, "uptown" tenth-generation Sephardic Jews, came to shop at an appetizing store on the Lower East Side run by Eastern European Jewish immigrants.

"My grandmother lived on the Upper East Side," she said, "on Park Avenue and Seventy-fourth Street. She was part of a very prominent family, and there was a room in Shearith Israel named after my grandfather, Louis Napoleon Levy. [*Who ever heard of a Jew named Napoleon?* I said to myself.] Occasionally she had me join her on trips to the Lower East Side, to places like Itzkowitz, the father-and-son pillow stuffers on Allen Street. We traveled in her chauffeur-driven limousine. There were no car heaters in those days, so she covered our legs with a mink lap robe. When we got to Itzkowitz, she gave them precise instructions on how the pillows were to be refilled. They promised to do the job within the hour, so then Granny took me to Russ & Daughters on Houston Street. Everybody knew about them. We picked out various kinds of smoked fish from the gleaming showcases. The counterman always gave us a taste [*That would have been my father,* I thought, *or one of my uncles; maybe even my grandfather*], and Granny bought a lot of fish. She said that she didn't come to the Lower East Side very often and that smoked fish kept well because of the smoke and the salt. I treasured those trips with Granny. I still come here, but now by bike from my house in Greenwich Village."

I was fascinated by her story. And how nice it was to find someone from a culture that was so very different from mine, for whom Russ & Daughters was also part of a treasured family memory.

The Other Holidays

At some point when I wasn't looking, Christmas and New Year's became Jewish holidays. The same number of customers coming in, the same amount of fish going out. I guess I had my head down, slicing and filleting, when it turned out that you don't have to be Jewish to love our food.

Here's the primary difference between Yom Kippur and Christmas: the crowd is much better behaved when buying for Christmas. They are about to engage in celebration, not deprivation. So the mood in the store—shared by customer and counterman—is a happy one. Though the lines and the wait time are just as long, there's no talk of jumping the line, and no one is due in surgery in an hour. And just for Christmas and New Year's we have an express line: the caviar express line.

The caviar express line is one of my finest creations, and perhaps one of my more notable legacies. The concept is to thin out the crowded store at Christmas and New Year's by expediting service to those who are prepared to spend a lot of money on a single small expensive item. Those who want smoked fish, herring, bagels, or all of the above must, as always, take a number and wait. Those who are buying only caviar zip right through on the express line. In my first year of retirement, my emeritus phase, I agreed to run the caviar express line. I also conscripted my new son-in-law, Christopher, to work with me. I no longer had the stamina—physical or mental—to work the counter, i.e., to handle the slicing, filleting, wrapping, packing, and schlepping. Christopher was raised in Ohio, which, correctly or not, I'd always thought of as part of the gastronomic wasteland known as Middle America. He was now in graduate school, studying to be a psychotherapist, and he had only recently learned about the products we carried. So the less-intense experience of the caviar express line was perfect for both of us.

Christopher watched and listened as I quickly moved the line of caviar-only customers, selling kilos, half-kilos, 250-gram tins, and

125-gram tins of American and Siberian osetra, with prices of the half-kilo tins running about a thousand dollars. When asked, I would explain the differences in flavor and texture of the various types of caviar. But it wasn't necessary to spend a lot of time with each customer because, having spent much of my life in retail, I could usually determine pretty quickly what a particular customer would like and could afford, and I would easily steer him or her to that choice. The customers were thankful for my advice and grateful not to have to wait on the long fish line.

Christopher assisted me with the first ten to fifteen sales by packing the caviar on ice, then in bags, and then ringing up the sale on the register as I moved on to the next customer. Then he stepped in to do the sales part himself, obviously to show me, his new father-in-law, that he could handle the task. I watched as he delivered long speeches extolling the virtues of the less-expensive caviars. I watched as customers whom I judged to be potential buyers of 250-gram tins of osetra bought 50-gram tins of paddlefish instead. He gave too much information, and the longer his monologues grew, the longer and more impatient the caviar express line grew. It was hardly express anymore. I watched, did my own selling, and kept my mouth shut. He was my new son-in-law. His wife—my daughter, Niki—was now running the business.

At some point during the process, as I redoubled my efforts if only to counterbalance my son-in-law's well-meaning but counterproductive strategy, I watched him wait on a rather distinguished-looking gentleman who asked for several hundred dollars' worth of osetra caviar. (I subsequently found out that this customer was a principal in a well-known New York art gallery.) The fellow was clearly in a rush and was therefore not subjected to Christopher's extended monologue. The caviar was brought out and packed on ice, and then I heard the gentleman ask Christopher, almost in a whisper, if it would be possible for him to also buy six plain bagels. Christopher, knowing full well that the caviar express line was only for caviar sales, looked over to me to see if I would grant his customer some papal in-law dispensation. I did. The customer was extremely pleased and thankful. Then, as he turned to leave, he said, "I only bought the caviar so that I wouldn't have to take a number and wait on line for the bagels."

On another occasion, one young man specifically waited for me to serve him on the caviar express line. He wanted my attention, which at that moment was divided among four or five customers. He offered to show me some magic tricks. I wasn't interested. I had to keep the caviar express line moving. He began doing the tricks anyway. He shoved a regular quarter into my hand, closed my fist, and the quarter bent like a pretzel. I was amazed. I started paying attention to him. Then he asked me to give him a twenty-dollar bill.

"No chance," I said. "I know you just want to beat me out of the twenty."

"No, seriously," he replied. "You've got to see this trick."

"Well, what's the harm," I said as I handed him a twenty-dollar bill. "If you steal my twenty, I'll just tack it onto your caviar bill."

And then, with some quick hand movements, my twenty did in fact disappear.

" I knew you'd do that. I can't believe I'm such a sucker."

"Look under your wristwatch band."

And there it was. I was dumbfounded. I had never seen such an amazing trick, even on TV.

"You know what?" I said. "You can give up your day job, whatever it is, and do magic for a living." I really meant it. This guy was good. There were some snickers from the crowd that had formed around him. Then Josh pulled me aside and told me that David Blaine was already one of the world's greatest magicians. David Blaine? Who knew?

And then there was the fellow standing quietly in the crowd.

"What do you do for a living?" I asked him as he waited for his number to be called. It's my normal opening gambit, a way to start the schmooze, and I'm always interested in what our customers do and where they live.

"I'm a writer."

"Oh, really?" I said, with the bravado of a newly published author. "Have you ever been published?" My one essay had recently appeared in a book called *Gastropolis.*

"I've done eight books with HarperCollins."

I was quickly put in my place. "What are your eight books about?" I asked, a bit more humbly.

"Sex."

There was no comeback for me here. This schmooze was over. I moved on to the next waiting customer.

Potato Latkes

MAKES 18 TO 20 LATKES

2½ pounds Idaho russet potatoes
1 medium onion
2 large eggs, separated
½ cup finely chopped scallions (white and green parts)
¼ cup potato flour or matzo meal
3 tablespoons unsalted butter, melted
2 teaspoons kosher salt
½ teaspoon freshly ground black pepper
¼ teaspoon baking powder
Canola or vegetable oil, for frying
Sour cream, for serving
Applesauce, for serving

Place a large strainer over a large bowl. Using the large holes of a box grater, grate some of the potatoes, followed by some of the onion, into the strainer. Repeat until all of the potatoes and onion are used up. (Alternating the potatoes and onion prevents the potatoes from discoloring.) Squeeze or press out as much of the liquid as possible. Allow the accumulated liquid to stand in another bowl for 2 to 3 minutes. Pour off the watery part but reserve the thick, starchy paste at the bottom.

Transfer the potato-onion mixture to a clean large bowl. Add the starchy paste, egg yolks, scallions, potato flour or matzo meal, butter, salt, pepper, and baking powder and mix well. In a separate medium bowl, beat the egg whites with an electric mixer until they hold stiff, shiny peaks. Fold the egg whites into the potato mixture.

Heat a thin layer of oil in a large frying pan over medium-high heat. Working in batches, scoop ¼ cup of the potato mixture into the pan for each pancake. Flatten gently with a spatula. Fry until the pancakes are crisp and golden brown, about 4 minutes per side.

Serve immediately or reheat in a 350°F oven for about 6 minutes. Serve with sour cream and applesauce.

8

The Business Model

Our Way

"*Nem a shmata und vishup da counter,*" Grandpa Russ would say in perfect Yinglish. Whether Grandpa Russ was concerned about dirt or about idle hands, "Pick up a rag and wipe off the counter" was Business Rule #1. It was passed down not only along the bloodlines to his daughters but also to their husbands, who then passed it along to the next generation.

Most people know the old adage "Cleanliness is next to godliness." But in the Russ family, cleanliness is above godliness. At Russ & Daughters, we were told, "You should be able to eat off the floor." Our employees have always worn spotless white coats, not aprons, when working behind the counter. White Formica and stainless steel, which were easy to keep clean, were the only acceptable materials for the showcases. Ancillary rules of cleanliness: "Never get caught with your hands in your pockets." "The only thing that goes into your pockets is a rag." "There is always something to be cleaned." Then there were the rest of the rules.

Rule #2: "Who's watching the register?" Rule #3: "There's no such thing as absentee ownership." In the Russ family, these rules were constantly repeated. Until credit cards arrived, Russ & Daughters was a cash business. And lots of cash in the register meant lots of temptation and lots of *tsuris.* Someone from the family always had to be within eyesight of the register in case an employee "made a mistake" while ringing up a sale or making change.

Although most purchases are now paid for with a credit or debit card, a Russ still must be in the store at all times, to make sure that "the merchandise is always rotated" (Rule #4) and, when necessary, to tell an employee to "drop what you're doing and take care of the customer" (Rule #5). "The customer is always right" is Rule #6, but it isn't chiseled in stone like the previous five rules. After all, in our store who knows more than we do about herring, smoked fish, and caviar?

The Handshake

Back in the old days, most people on the Lower East Side did business with a simple handshake. No one knows when that tradition ended and the my-lawyer-will-call-your-lawyer business model began. Sometimes I wonder if Grandpa Russ had something to do with that.

I have known the Yavarkovsky family since I was born. They owned and ran a paper-goods business out of a few small warehouses on Ludlow Street, one block from Russ & Daughters. Above one of the warehouses was a dentist's office in the front (for one of the Yavarkovsky sons) and an apartment in the back. That was where we lived when I was born, in September 1945.

Rose Yavarkovsky, a longtime fixture on the Lower East Side, the daughter of pushcart peddlers, married the Yavarkovsky son who took over the family business. When he died, Rose ran the business herself, and later ran it with one of her sons. It's hard to tell how old Rose is. She admits to being in her nineties. But Aunt Hattie says, "She's a few years older than me," and Aunt Hattie is now ninety-nine.

Until recently, Rose stood outside her warehouses on Ludlow Street each day, rain or shine (wearing a mink coat in the winter), clipboard in hand, checking in merchandise that arrived in large trailer trucks from the paper-goods manufacturers and checking out merchandise being picked up by small jobbers and retailers in their cars and vans.

Conversations with Rose were civil and usually about business; we weren't friends. If we didn't pay within two weeks for paper goods that we'd purchased for the store, I'd get a reminder call from her. On a recent shopping trip to Russ & Daughters, Rose seemed chattier than usual and anxious to tell me a story about Grandpa Russ, whom she referred to as Yoi'el (she used the Eastern European pronunciation), and her father-in-law, Joseph (for him she used the American pronunciation).

My mom and me in front of the warehouse building on Ludlow Street

As Rose recounted the story, Grandpa Russ bought paper bags and wax paper for wrapping smoked fish from Joseph Yavarkovsky for many years. One time, Yoi'el needed to borrow some money, so he went to Joseph, who loaned him the money at no interest, to be repaid on a certain day. They shook hands. According to Rose, when the due date came, Yoi'el didn't repay the loan and didn't say anything about repaying it. So Joseph went to Yoi'el to ask for his money back. Yoi'el was offended that anyone should ask him, Yoi'el Russ, to repay a loan, knowing that his word was as good as gold and that he would, of course, repay it as soon as he had the money. *Shtolts* was the word that

Rose used to describe Yoi'el. Literally translated from the Yiddish, it means "proud," but it was clear that she meant "arrogant."

Yoi'el ultimately repaid the loan, but he never forgot the slight to his honor. A few years later, Joseph wanted to buy a small one-story warehouse at 183 Ludlow Street that Yoi'el owned and used to store wooden barrels filled with herring. The property was near the two warehouses Joseph already owned, and he wanted a third. Even though Yoi'el needed the money, he would never, "not over my dead body," sell it to the offensive Joseph Yavarkovsky. "Big shot," he sneered. "Who does he think he is?"

According to Rose, her father-in-law then engaged the services of an Italian lawyer, whom he sent to Yoi'el with a shopping bag full of cash and a claim that his client was an Italian grocer. Yoi'el sold the property, not knowing that the ultimate purchaser was Joseph Yavarkovsky. We don't know what happened when Grandpa Russ found out, but I'm glad I wasn't there when he did.

Rose told me she had just sold the three tiny warehouses on Ludlow Street to a developer who planned to build a sixteen-story boutique hotel on the site. Her price was $13.5 million, she said with a wry smile. As an afterthought, she mentioned that for years the paper goods stored in the warehouse that her father-in-law bought from my grandfather reeked of herring, which caused many complaints from their customers. So the Russes had the last laugh. And the Yavarkovskys have $13.5 million. Aunt Hattie, who had never heard about any of this, ascribes what she considers Rose's tall tale to jealousy. "After all," she said, "Rose was the daughter of peddlers who sold onions and potatoes, and their pushcart stood for years in the street right in front of Russ & Daughters."

Changing the Business Model

When I arrived on the scene in 1978 to take over the business, it was clear that some things had to change. Grandpa Russ's preferred business model—*etzel-petzel* (seat-of-the-pants)—had been in place since he first opened the store. As far as I know, this approach to running a retail outlet is not taught in business schools. I would be the one to turn Russ & Daughters into a real business.

Before the Yom Kippur holiday rush during my first year in the store, I discovered that there had never been a real attempt to implement a method to maintain crowd control and customer flow. Grandpa Russ, my parents, and my uncles and aunts felt that having customers take a number from a machine and wait their turn was insulting, impersonal, and too "uptown." So a system was developed, and it was followed whether there was a holiday or not, whether there were two or two hundred customers in the store. It was known as the "CU" system in shorthand; in longhand it was "See-You," and it went like this: Each working member of the family had his or her own following of customers. When regular customers came into the store, family members would recognize them and know who usually took care of them (even if, more often than not, their names would not be remembered). And so the word would go out to the appropriate Russ, "Herbie, your CU is here!" This was understood to be the Russ & Daughters way of doing business.

Those who did not have a CU would wait for the call "Who's next?" Inevitably, the same response came simultaneously from several elderly ladies, who answered with a phrase no longer used today but very common in the argot of the Lower East Side of the past: "My next!"

That Yom Kippur eve I watched in disbelief as three women simultaneously shouted "My next!" in response to the counterman's call. The rest of the waiting customers spontaneously divided themselves into three groups, each one allying with and arguing on behalf of the contestant who they believed was entitled to be waited on next. It was not a pretty scene. Besides being an affront to my sense of professionalism, this situation was also commercially unworkable. It meant all business came to a dead stop, which meant time and money were being wasted.

I went to the office in back of the store, found a package of index cards, and numbered each card from 1 through 100. I took numbers 1, 2, and 3 and randomly gave one to each of the "My Nexts." (They didn't complain; they saw the determined look in my eyes.) I put the remaining cards in a plastic pickle container and insisted that each of the other customers take a number with some sense of honor for the order in which they came into the store.

The customers comprehended the gravity of the situation and knew they had to be flexible, or they would leave without their smoked fish for the break-fast. They quickly organized themselves and took numbers.

It was another matter for the customers who came in later and who hadn't witnessed the mayhem or been part of its resolution. They required explanations and some convincing, especially the "celebrities" who had never taken a number anywhere for any reason and the "old-time regulars" who couldn't understand what had happened, since my grandparents, parents, aunts, and uncles had never asked them to do anything so bizarre as to wait their turn or take a number.

But from then on, customers who came into Russ & Daughters took a number from a little red machine (the pickle container gave things a nice homey touch, but it wasn't a very efficient number dispenser) and waited their turn. The "CU" system was no longer an option: there were no longer three Russ daughters and three Russ sons-in-law to divvy up the customers. I was the only Russ behind the counter for a long time.

From Mom and Pop to What?

One day I heard my father on the phone with some Hollywood movie mogul who wanted several pounds of sturgeon and smoked salmon shipped to him for a party the following week. "Sure," I heard my father say. "Send me a check and when it clears the bank, I'll send you the fish." This method of order fulfillment could take several weeks, so the movie mogul got his fish somewhere else, somewhere more accommodating, more trusting.

This was long before synthetic ice gels, insulated Styrofoam boxes, FedEx overnight shipping, and, most important, credit cards. My grandfather, my parents, and my aunts and uncles were cautious people who had lived through the Great Depression. They knew that even "the biggest"—doctors, lawyers, Hollywood moguls—could bounce checks. And once a check bounced, there was the inevitable awkwardness of trying to get the no-goodnik on the phone—maybe several calls would be necessary—to get him to "make good" on the "rubber."

Of course, such phone calls would inevitably lead to losing the customer, who was either too embarrassed or too offended that the fish man would bother them over a bounced check.

I didn't need an MBA to change and improve shipping at Russ & Daughters. Credit cards and overnight deliveries did that. But I did need help to institute an ambitious change in management style—if we even had one at all. I wanted to go from a mom-and-pop, *etzel-petzel* company to something that vaguely resembled an actual business. My first and biggest challenge was our employees. Starting with me.

I was increasingly unhappy with the role I was playing, or perhaps had created for myself, at the store—being responsible for just about everything. The hardest task was managing employees whose interests were not always the same as mine. Grandpa Russ's challenge had been different: he had a family that acted like employees. My energies were devoted to getting employees to act like family, to firing and to hiring from a shrinking labor pool, and to supervising and motivating.

Keeping the employees happy often meant dealing with their personal problems: an unhappy marriage, crushing child-support payments, unpaid debts, substance abuse. Too often I returned to the role of lawyer to untangle an employee's legal mess. And all this was on top of my everyday role in the store as teacher, psychologist, father figure, taskmaster, and dispenser of rewards and punishments.

In an attempt to extricate myself from this situation, I hired a business consultant, a sharply dressed, preppy-looking young man who had no familiarity with our type of small retail business and had never been inside an appetizing store before. He made up for his lack of experience with an infectious optimism and self-confidence. He claimed to be a disciple of a person he referred to as "the great Edwards Deming." I had absolutely no idea who Edwards Deming was. Turns out he was a business management guru who singlehandedly turned around the postwar economy of Japan and changed the perception of "Made in Japan" from inferior goods to quality products. His methodology was taught at Harvard Business School. So, over the objection of my business partner—my wife, Maria, who thought the whole idea was stupid—I hired this young consultant at great expense.

Maria; our store manager, Herman; and I attended many meetings with our consultant to get management on the same page with respect to goals and methods. Then a series of meetings was held with everyone else in attendance—our staff of lox slicers and kitchen workers. The concept was to motivate employees so that management emerged from the bottom up rather than from the top down. Everyone, no matter what their job, should be invested in quality control and in productive operations in a happy work environment. The means of getting to our desired goals required an understanding of flowcharts, bone charts, operating manuals, organization tables, mission statements, and checklists. At the end of each meeting, everyone counted to three and clapped their hands. If this happened in unison, it was evidence that we were coming together as a group and that we would quickly and easily achieve our goals.

After a year of weekly meetings and many thousands of dollars paid to our consultant, we had pretty well mastered the in-unison handclap. But Maria was right: most of the staff never understood what flowcharts, bone charts, mission statements, and operational manuals had to do with slicing lox or filleting herrings. And I was still responsible for everything.

Special Projects

In March 2001 Niki came to work with us at Russ & Daughters. Niki and Maria formed an alliance: "From now on," they told me, "Niki will be in charge of special projects." Russ & Daughters never had someone in charge of special projects. I didn't even know what "special projects" meant, unless it referred to someone calling up and wanting two hundred schmaltz herrings cleaned, filleted, and ready for pickup in an hour.

I wanted Niki to learn the business the way I had—by working the counter for ten hours a day, six days a week, slicing lox and filleting herrings, filling in the showcase, making salads in the kitchen, whatever it took. In my head she was the heir apparent and would ultimately run the store, but she couldn't supervise our employees unless she knew what they were supposed to do, when they were supposed to do it, how they were supposed to do it, and how long it should take.

When I first came into the business, I had fierce arguments with my father about whether I would work five days a week (my preference) or six days (his, of course). The ten-hour days were a given; I didn't even bother to bring that up. But to my father the workweek issue was nonnegotiable. I ended up working six days a week, ten hours a day, with two weeks' vacation a year, for many years. I thought Niki should do the same. Maria and Niki disagreed. I knew I was going to lose this one; that alliance was too strong. As a compromise, Niki worked behind the counter when the store was very busy; otherwise she applied herself to "special projects," which turned out to be the development of a website and Internet shipping business. This took a bit of getting used to on my part, I have to admit.

Now, when I turned on my computer, orders suddenly and magically appeared on the screen: orders from people I didn't know, living in places I'd never heard of. It was terrifying. This wasn't the way the Russ family did business. If you wanted to buy our fish, you came to the store. If you wanted to place an order over the phone, we had to recognize your voice or know your family. ("My grandmother is Rose Cohen. She told me you'd take care of me.") Once again, I was just hopelessly out of date. Internet sales are now a very substantial part of our business.

Josh was a little more agreeable to learning the business the old-fashioned way. I spent several years teaching him the Russ business model: Stand behind the counter and always keep a rag in your pocket and your eyes on everything. He was a quick learner, a product of his training as an engineer, no doubt. But my appreciation for Josh and his linear style was put to the test when he approached me one day about investing in a POS system.

I tried to keep an open mind. After all, I had pooh-poohed Niki's idea to set up a website some years before and was wrong on that one. But this project seemed different. POS is an acronym for "point-of-sale." Josh wanted to install a computerized sales and inventory management system. I am always suspicious of acronyms, which have the tendency to make difficult and complex matters seem almost babyishly easy and thereby lead the user into a deep, dark, and expensive hole. This project was going to be very expensive. It was also too high-tech for me. People of my age are the cyber-cusp generation. If we have not yet begun our descent into pre-senile dementia, we are able to use the computer for such basic functions as word processing, e-mailing, Googling, and solitaire. Anything beyond that is probably incomprehensible or, at best, a struggle. So the concept of many computers, cash registers, and scales somehow linked together to form an integrated system that would keep track of our inventory was both awesome and terrifying.

My primary concern—putting aside my technophobia—was whether this POS system made sense, given the low-tech, labor-intensive nature of our business and the perishable products sold in our traditional and historic little appetizing store. Would this system mean that Niki, Josh, and I would be spending more time in the office and less on the floor watching the products, the employees, and the customers? Would each minute spent in front of the computer mean one less minute to see if the herrings on the bottom layer of the showcase were being rotated to the top? One less minute to notice that a highly paid salmon slicer has, for lack of attention, cut too thick a slice and thrown his mistake in the garbage? One less minute to observe a customer's body language and reaction to a sample taste of a newly created item?

I was too attached to the "old days, old ways" of doing business to make a dispassionate decision on this POS issue. Grandpa Russ, in his first and only renovation of the store, around 1950, designed an office in the back that measures five feet by seven feet and has barely enough room for one person and one desk. The walls don't meet the ceiling, and the office is next to the hot and noisy kitchen. There's a glass-paned window but no lock on the door. It's not a place where you'd want to spend a significant amount of time. But that was okay with Grandpa Russ. To his way of thinking, one couldn't be in the office and keep an eye on the registers at the same time. I suppose that's how I felt, too. I wasn't enthusiastic about POS, so I let Josh and Niki make the decision about whether to install it.

I was wrong. Again. The POS system freed the Russes from laborious, time-sucking paperwork and tasks such as figuring out sales volume and tracking inventory. The bottom line is that it allowed us to spend *less* time in the office and *more* time in the store with our products, employees, and customers.

. . .

Lessons were learned. It was possible to make the business more efficient, more productive, and more profitable. The fourth generation of Russes was well positioned and had the educational background to make the necessary changes. In addition to the website and the POS system, Niki and Josh started a blog called Lox Populi, which keeps people in the loop about all things related to Russ & Daughters. Our customers love it. Russ & Daughters can also be followed on Twitter and Tumblr, which I'm sure I'd find impressive if I could figure out what Twitter and Tumblr are. One thing I *was* sure of: the business was moving beyond my ability to control it, or even to understand how to operate it. I was becoming a dinosaur. It was time for me to get out of the way.

Josh, Herman, and Niki with Hannah Milman and Martha Stewart
(Courtesy of Martha Stewart Living Omnimedia, Inc.)

Bagel Chips

YIELDS 48 TO 60 CHIPS

6 day-old bagels, preferably a mix of plain, poppy, sesame, and pumpernickel
¼ cup extra-virgin olive oil
2 teaspoons kosher salt
1 teaspoon garlic powder
½ teaspoon freshly ground black pepper

Position racks in the upper and lower thirds of the oven and preheat it to 325°F. Line two baking sheets with parchment paper.

Using a sharp serrated knife, slice the bagels as thinly as possible into *O*'s. You should have 8 to 10 slices per bagel. Divide the bagels between the baking sheets, spreading them in an even layer. Using a pastry brush, brush the olive oil in a thin layer over the bagels. Combine the salt, garlic powder, and pepper in a small bowl. Sprinkle evenly over the bagels.

Bake the bagels until they are just beginning to turn golden brown, 7 to 10 minutes. Remove the baking sheets from the oven and flip the bagel chips over. Return the baking sheets to the oven, reversing their positions so that the one that was on the bottom is now on the top, and continue to bake until the chips are golden brown and crisp, about 5 minutes more.

Taste the chips and adjust the seasonings, adding more salt, pepper, and garlic powder if necessary. Cool the chips completely on wire racks.

Bagel Pudding with Prunes and Raisins

SERVES 6 TO 8

3 large eggs
1 large egg yolk
1 cup sugar
1 tablespoon pure vanilla extract
¼ teaspoon ground cinnamon
2 cups half-and-half
1 cup whole milk
4 to 5 day-old plain bagels, crusts removed and cut into ½-inch cubes (about 8 cups)
1¼ cups pitted prunes, halved
¾ cup seedless black raisins
Confectioners' sugar

Whisk the eggs, egg yolk, sugar, vanilla, and cinnamon in a large bowl until smooth. Whisk in the half-and-half and milk. Add the bagel cubes and toss to coat. Allow the mixture to stand, stirring occasionally, until the bagel cubes have absorbed most of the liquid, about 1 hour.

Position a rack in the middle of the oven and preheat it to 325°F. Grease a 9-by-9-inch baking dish or spray it with nonstick spray. Stir the prunes and raisins into the bagel mixture. Transfer the mixture to the prepared dish and pour any remaining liquid over the top. Bake for 50 minutes to 1 hour, until the top is golden brown and a tester inserted in the center comes out clean. If the top is browning too quickly, tent it with aluminum foil. Cool the bagel pudding completely on a wire rack, then dust with confectioners' sugar.

9

The Legacy

A Burden or a Blessing; Kvetch *or* Kvell

It seems that not too long ago I was considered by my customers, my employees, and my suppliers to be "the kid." As in "Hey, kid, I want the same kind of sturgeon your mother gave me." Or "Hey, kid, your father and uncles always paid their bills within a week. It's ten days. Whassup over there?" But now I am one of the old men in the ever-shrinking world of appetizing. I am officially retired, except for writing this book (which, I've discovered, is harder than selling retail) and adopting the mantle of schmoozer in chief.

I have passed our family business on to the fourth generation of Russes—my nephew and my daughter. This is what I call success: the ultimate validation of having the next generation want to do what you have done most of your life. What words of wisdom can I impart? What direction can I provide as a path to success? How can they benefit from my experience when their own experiences will bring different challenges? A neighborhood that has gone from pushcart to posh; a customer base that has evolved from Jewish and local to ethnically mixed, urbane, young, and far-flung; a labor force that continues to change, reflecting our nation's immigration patterns; and an ever-evolving display of products: the old familiar ones that change with the times or that disappear entirely, and the new ones that keep our business fresh and relevant. Perhaps I can show them where the minefields are hidden, having stepped on quite a few of them along the way. But I cannot give them advice about a future I do not fully understand. They are better educated and better equipped than I am to take Russ & Daughters into the twenty-first century. So what's left for me to teach them? Our *yichis.* A trip to Beth David Cemetery in Elmont, New York, is in order.

Location, Location, Location

As far as graves are concerned, the Russ family plot on the corner of Mount Judah and Washington Avenues in Beth David Cemetery is as good a piece of property as you can get. Besides being in a corner spot, it contains an old yet still vibrant oak tree, a breath of life in an otherwise lifeless community. Under the tree there's a stone bench with enough room for three Russes to sit comfortably in the shade and gossip about the more permanent inhabitants.

"You'll come *mit der kinder,* haf a *bissel* to eat, make a wisit. Plenty room, you'll enjoy." In 1955, that's how Joel Russ explained his most recent real estate purchase to his three daughters. They understood that the room he was talking about was not a new house but the twenty-nine grave sites in this shaded corner plot, enough for him and Bella, their three daughters and their husbands, the seven grandchildren and their future husbands and wives, with a little left over. "What's not to like?"

This real estate purchase was one of many that Grandpa Russ made without first consulting his family. Over the years, not even his wife knew where or when they would next move. How many attempts did he make to get the family out of the Lower East Side until he finally succeeded? His daughters said there were "too many to remember." When asked if they ever objected to this authoritarian decision making, they replied, "Papa knew best" and "Papa was always trying to do better." They never thought that this might be Papa's attempt to keep control of the family—even from the grave.

This visit to Beth David is Niki's and Josh's first. It provides the appropriate backdrop for my delivery of the speech I have been preparing for the past few years as the business transitioned from the third generation (me) to the fourth generation (them). They should know where the Russes come from, about our struggles along the way, and about our failures and successes. They haven't yet been beaten up by the world of retail. They haven't had to deal with competition from an appetizing store on every block. They haven't spent years waiting for

My mom and dad, behind the counter

customers to trickle in from uptown and the outer boroughs while our own neighborhood was drowning in crime and drugs. They haven't had to take money from their own pockets to make payroll when the city dug up the street in front of our store in the middle of the Great Depression.

I tell them about my first visit here, under somewhat different circumstances. When I left the law firm where I was a litigator to join the family business, I expected a less hectic, more meaningful life. Instead, I was soon overwhelmed by the constant petty annoyances, stresses, and hardships of retail, by having to stand on my feet behind the counter ten hours a day, six days a week, waiting on some of New York's most difficult customers. This was nothing like practicing law. That was a piece of cake compared to this.

One day as I stood behind the counter, I made the mistake of complaining to my father. "When do I get a rest?" I asked.

Rather unceremoniously, my dad grabbed me by the arm, took me outside to the car, and proceeded to drive without saying where we were going and, indeed, without saying another word. En route, he lit up one of his omnipresent cigars. I learned from an early age that my father could never be separated from his cigars, not at any time or under any circumstances, not even while traveling in a car in the winter with the windows closed and his three kids retching in the backseat. But by the time we made this trip I had become a cigarette smoker, so I lit up, too, and we continued our journey in a fog of smoke and silence. We neared the Belmont Park racetrack. This looked promising. But then we passed the track and drove through the gates of Beth David Cemetery to the Russ family plot, which was then populated only by Joel and Bella Russ. My father finally spoke.

"You want a rest? *This* is the only place you'll get it!" Then we left and returned to the store. Nothing else was said.

My next visit to the family plot at Beth David was two years later. "There's a new inhabitant arriving," I tell Josh and Niki, "my father, your grandfather." He was sixty years old when he died, felled by the eighth heart attack he'd had over the course of eighteen years. We hadn't had much time together for him to teach me the business. For the last two years of his life he had been living in Florida, where he had been forced to retire shortly after I arrived at Russ & Daughters. "You need to rest," his doctors had said.

Today the family plot is more heavily populated. Grandpa and Grandma Russ are still in the center. Aunt Ida, the middle Russ daughter and the only one who believed in an afterlife, has a place next to the father with whom she fought all of her life. Who knows what's going on with them now? Three sons-in-law—my father and my two uncles—are all there. My cousin Nina recently joined them. That makes seven out of twenty-nine grave sites occupied. There's still "plenty room."

I walk Josh and Niki several cemetery blocks over to one of the community burial grounds maintained by a *landsmanshaft,* a dues-paying mutual aid society formed by immigrants who came from the same shtetl. The *landsmanshaft*'s main purpose was to help families in need; to help, for example, a young widow bury her husband and feed her children until she was able to get back on her feet.

"Your great-grandfather," I explain, "was from a shtetl called Strzyzov. It was a tiny town in Galicia, in what's now southeastern Poland.

"Grandpa Russ was a member of the Strzyzover Landsmanshaft, and he and his family could have been buried in plots that the society owned," I tell them, "but he chose not to. Owning his own family plot would be a testament to his success in America and would show that he didn't need a helping hand from a *landsmanshaft.* He could afford a corner plot with a big oak tree, a stone bench, and room for many generations of Russes. This was America, where with hard work and determination there was no limit to what a person could achieve. Grandpa Russ wanted his descendants to understand this even after he was long gone. That was why he wanted there to be a place in the Russ family plot where we could come for a 'wisit'—not to say prayers, but to sit on the bench, have something to eat, and remember where we come from."

The business Grandpa Russ founded with a pushcart, expanded with a horse and wagon, and finally established as a store he decided to call Russ & Daughters is now famous. We're still on the Lower East Side. But what we have been doing here all of these years has become of interest to the larger world.

In 2001, the Smithsonian Institution invited us to participate in a special exhibition about New York City. "You're part of New York's cultural heritage," they wrote. And in 2005, the Smithsonian invited us to be part of another exhibit, this time saying, "You're part of the food culture of America." I couldn't help thinking about how Grandpa Russ would regard all of this. "So, *nu*?" he'd say with a smile and a shrug. "We're finally real Americans."

Perhaps the greatest acknowledgment of our *yichis* came from the Museum of Jewish Heritage in New York. The museum presents an annual spring program of events that involves lectures by renowned figures—writers, artists, and performers—in the world of Jewish culture. In the winter of 2003, the museum called Niki and invited Russ & Daughters to participate in one such event. I overheard Niki promise them the participation of three generations of the Russ family, including the two surviving Russ daughters—her grandmother Anne (who was then eighty-two) and her great-aunt Hattie (who was then ninety). I also heard her offer the services of the noted author and humorist Calvin Trillin as moderator for the event. She got off the phone very pleased with herself. I immediately pointed out the logistical problems.

First, it was an extraordinary leap of faith and some chutzpah for her to presume that Calvin Trillin would agree to appear. Second, it was rather unlikely that her grandmother and aunt would be willing to travel to New York for this event, since they were both more or less under self-imposed house arrest in their Florida shtetl. Although they both had valid driver's licenses and their own cars, they rarely logged more than a few hundred miles a year, using their cars only for trips to the hairdresser, to the Publix supermarket, and, most often, to their doctors.

"Niki," I said, "I'll call your grandmother to see what I can do. But there's no way I can call Bud Trillin for this. You'll have to take care of that yourself."

I didn't expect success on either front, and I wondered which one of us would have to call the museum to say we couldn't pull the event together.

Bud Trillin said yes right away. As is evident from the beautiful foreword he wrote for this book, he's a longtime customer and good friend, and we consider him the poet laureate of Russ & Daughters. He's also particularly fond of Niki, which I completely understand. She's much more adorable than I am. And at a time when his own two daughters were off living in California, he was vulnerable.

My mother presented more of a challenge. "Mom," I said, "there's a museum here in New York that wants to feature our store and our family at an event in the spring. Do you think you and Aunt Hattie can make it?"

Jews are famous for our ability to answer one question with another, and my mother is a master of this. "What do I need this for?" she sighed. "Can't they come here? Why would a museum want us? How much will it cost?"

Once she finished her *shpiel,* I told her that whatever reasons the museum might have, this event would be "good for business." She got it. The Russ entrepreneurial DNA kicked in, and she was immediately on board. But she then came up with a list of demands befitting a rock star: a limousine to take her and Hattie to and from the airport. Wheelchairs for both of them. First-class tickets. A luxury hotel in New York—four stars at least. To my surprise, the museum agreed to it all. (It turned out the limousine was a minivan, the first-class seats were by the bulkhead in coach, and the luxury hotel was an Embassy Suites, but Mom and Aunt Hattie were by then too thrilled with the whole idea of the event to notice.) Some months before our scheduled event, the museum advertised its entire spring program of ten events in *The New York Times.* Our evening was billed as "A Talk Across Generations: Three Generations of the Russ & Daughters Family in Conversation with Calvin Trillin." When the ad appeared a second time, only the Russ & Daughters event had a bold black line through it with the words "Sold Out." It's impossible to tell whether the crowd showed up for Calvin Trillin, for the Russ family, or for the bagels and lox served after the talk, but for Aunt Hattie and my mom, the evening was the ultimate payback for a lifetime of hard, uncelebrated work. It was their evening of *koved*—respect, honor, esteem.

Onstage, Anne and Hattie did what they always do; they argued. When did Papa buy the building from Mrs. Franck? When did sister Ida leave the business? What was the price of sturgeon in 1939? They were unfazed by the several hundred people in the audience listening to them. As they argued, Niki, Josh, and I, sitting up there on the stage with them, watched the smiling faces of the audience members, who were delighted to see the "Russ girls reminiscing."

Anchor and Weight

The lament of the ancient Jewish retailer: "The first generation founds the business, the second generation builds the business, and the third generation kills the business."

At Russ & Daughters, I am that third generation, and by the grace of God and a lot of hard work, I haven't killed the business; it has survived and in fact thrived, and so have I. For all the changes we have experienced in our appetizing store on the Lower East Side, the one thing that hasn't changed, that is immutable, is the fear. The fear of being the last generation to run Russ & Daughters, the generation that "killed the business." How? By violating traditions, by tinkering with something that appears to be working just fine. If some product or way of displaying it is changed, or some way of doing business is changed, one or more of three things might happen: (1) it might bring on the *kaynahora* (the evil eye). Or, worse yet, (2) the wrath of our predecessors, the first- and second-generation Russes, either from beyond the grave or from Florida. Even more catastrophic would be (3) the disappointment and probable loss of customers who expect things to be done the "Russ" way, the way they have always been done by the previous generations of Russes. If the way they did business had worked, then what right did the new generation have to change it?

But some changes are necessary, forced on us by factors outside our

Russ & Daughters today

control. And some traditions can be traps, tethering us to ways of doing business that no longer work. Making those changes that are necessary to remain in business and jettisoning those traditions that would turn Russ & Daughters into a museum rather than a vibrant place of business is the burden of the next generation. Keeping one foot in the shtetl and the other in cyberspace is indeed a challenge for Niki and Josh, but one that they are more than qualified to meet.

Sometimes I think I stayed in the business as long as I did just to hear our customers tell us their stories about Russ & Daughters. With our food they celebrate births, mourn the loss of loved ones, and commemorate every major event in between. We have grown to know them and their families over the years, and even the generations. What a joy to prepare platters for the wedding of a customer whose bris and bar mitzvah we also catered. What heartache when we must deliver shiva platters to a family whose loved one, a friend and customer for so many years, has passed away. Sometimes Russ & Daughters is even mentioned in their eulogies. What a bittersweet honor. And what a pleasure it is for us to know that when friends and family gather, they want to mark the occasion with food from Russ & Daughters.

These traditions are a blessing, one that I hope will someday touch my three granddaughters—the fifth-generation Russes. It won't be too long before they are teething on bagels, then noshing on cream cheese and lox, and then maybe having a bite of herring. Perhaps someday they'll take their place behind the counter, having learned how to tell good fish from bad, how to treat customers, and how to keep the countertops sparkling clean.

We're proud that Russ & Daughters is different from the rest of the food world. We're not an impersonal big-box store; we don't sell mass-produced, extruded and preformed, prepackaged products. We live and breathe the most important Russ family traditions—a passion for what we sell and a dedication to providing the best possible service to our customers. All of this will, I hope, continue to keep Russ & Daughters a beloved part of New York's cultural and gastronomic life, and of the cyber world of gourmet food. Besides, as Grandpa Russ would say, *Vi nempt men parnosa?* How else are we going to make a living?

Lox Chowder

YIELDS 4 TO 6 SERVINGS

1 tablespoon extra-virgin olive oil
1 tablespoon unsalted butter
2 medium leeks, diced, white parts only (about 2 cups)
1 medium carrot, diced
2 small stalks celery, diced
1 clove garlic, minced
1 large russet potato, peeled and cut into ½-inch cubes (about 2 cups)
2 teaspoons minced fresh thyme
¼ cup all-purpose flour
¼ cup dry white wine
2 cups low-sodium chicken stock
1 bay leaf
2 cups whole milk
4 ounces smoked salmon, flaked (use the collar and wings if possible)
¾ cup heavy cream
Kosher salt
Freshly ground black pepper
Minced fresh chives, for garnish

Heat the olive oil and butter in a large, heavy-bottomed stockpot over medium heat. Add the leeks, carrot, and celery, and sauté until the vegetables have softened, about 5 minutes. Add the garlic, potato, and thyme and sauté until the garlic is fragrant, about 2 minutes more (be careful not to brown the garlic). Sprinkle the flour over the vegetables and stir well to create a dry roux. Stir in the wine, chicken stock, and bay leaf and bring the mixture to a simmer. Simmer until the potato cubes are tender when pierced with a fork, 30 to 35 minutes. Stir in the milk and salmon and return the mixture to a gentle simmer (do not boil).

Remove and discard the bay leaf. Stir in the cream and season to taste with salt and pepper. Garnish with the minced chives.

ACKNOWLEDGMENTS

I love people and I love telling stories. And for the thirty years that I ran Russ & Daughters, every day brought me new people and new stories. But telling a story across the counter is a lot easier than putting it into written words. I am not a natural writer. Writing, I have found, is harder than retail. So I needed just the right people along the way to encourage, edit, and nurse me through this process and project. They are all dear friends.

Dr. Annie Hauck-Lawson and Dr. Jonathan Deutsch must take the blame for first bringing me into the world of writing by inviting me to be a contributor to their wonderful food anthology, *Gastropolis: Food and New York City.* Annie coined the phrase and developed the concept of the "food voice," and she helped me find mine.

Larry Freundlich is one of the smartest and most righteous people I know. He encouraged me to write this book, and he made me believe that the stories I had to tell were worth telling and had meaning beyond the family fish store. Alfred Gingold, author and actor, has a pitch-perfect ear for a punch line. If I made him laugh, the story stayed in.

Emily Forland has been the perfect agent. Wise beyond her years, she helped put the proposal together and sell the book, and she guided me every step of the way. She knows her business. Sometimes I would call her just to *kvetch.* She handled me with great equanimity and greater insight.

It is with Harriet Bell that I spent the most time throughout the writing process. On a daily basis, sometimes several times a day, we would bandy about words and ideas. I call her my "collaborator," though she hates the word and says it conjures up visions of Vichy France. She is the ultimate professional, and I quickly came to understand and appreciate her ability and judgment. Harriet has helped to turn my sometimes ponderous ramblings into something readable, a book. Though she comes from Ohio, she shares my New York–centric view of the world and my Jewish sense of humor.

Niki is my daughter first but in this case an editor as well. Having Niki review and participate in the editing of this book had the potential for conflict, but she was graceful, gracious, and intelligent in her editorial suggestions. She shares my passion for the store and the stories.

Altie Karper of Schocken Books is my editor and publisher. She bought my book, polished and refined it, and produced the end product that you now hold in your hands and that I am proud to display in our store's window and on our counter (next to the rugelach and above the herrings). From the beginning, Altie understood me, my store, and my story because we share a similar background; she is a denizen of the Lower East Side with an important pedigree: her grandparents had a poultry store on Cannon Street. Altie and me, it's a *shidduch* made in heaven: the Herring Man and the Chicken Lady.

Matt Hranek is the photographer's photographer. To have his beautiful pictures of our food in this book requires a special thanks. And thanks to Lucy Baker for translating the huge scale of our recipes into a form useful for consumers. My thanks also to the scholars and historians who generously shared their time, research, and knowledge: Jane Ziegelman of the Lower East Side Tenement Museum, Suzanne Wasserman of the Gotham Center for New York City History, Rebecca Federman of the New York Public Library, and Eric Ferrara of the Lower East Side History Project. For sharing their knowledge of fish facts and fish lore, my thanks to the fish smokers Dave Sklar of Nova Scotia Food Products, Eric Kaslow of Acme Smoked Fish, Avi Attias of Banner Smoked Fish, and Harvey Oxenberg of Florida Smoked Fish. To Jerry Rumain, a scholar of the human psyche, thank you for your guidance and wisdom from the beginning.

All of the customers who listened to my stories and told me theirs must be acknowledged as well. They are too numerous to list, but special thanks go to Ruth Tanenbaum Shapiro, Nancy Bookman Goldman, Phyllis Flood Feder, Andrew Feuerstein, and Nancy Kramer, who provided such touching remembrances.

My thanks to all of the members of the Russ & Daughters staff, who grew up with me in the business and who have become my extended family—especially to Herman Vargas and José Reyes, Russes not by birth but by dedication, passion, and hard work.

Finally, this is, after all, a book about a family business, where whatever lines exist between family and business are most often blurry at best. I have dedicated the book to my mother and my aunts, the Russ Daughters, but it is their husbands—my father and my uncles—who wound up doing the yeoman's work of getting the right fish into the store and then into the hands and homes of the customers, ten hours a day, six days a week. Similarly, my wife, Maria, found that she had married not only me but the business as well, and she took her place in the store not just in a supporting role but as a lead actor and as a star. For the past forty years she has been my true partner in both the family and the business. Our son, Noah, did not come into the business. He followed his dream of becoming a doctor and is now a pediatric oncologist at UCLA. He works long hours, very hard, and with great passion. It is in his DNA. I'm proud of him.

And last but not least, I am happy to acknowledge and express my gratitude to the fourth generation at Russ & Daughters—my daughter, Niki, and my nephew Josh. They had the education and the ability to do whatever they wanted in the world of work, and they willingly and enthusiastically chose a life behind the counter of our store. I am delighted and proud. The fish continues to be great, and the stories continue to be told.

A NOTE ABOUT THE TYPE

This book was set in Adobe Garamond. Designed for the Adobe Corporation by Robert Slimbach, the fonts are based on types first cut by Claude Garamond (c. 1480–1561). Garamond was a pupil of Geoffroy Tory and is believed to have followed the Venetian models, although he introduced a number of important differences, and it is to him that we owe the letter we now know as "old style."

Typeset by North Market Street Graphics,
Lancaster, Pennsylvania

Printed and bound by Berryville Graphics,
Berryville, Virginia

Designed by M. Kristen Bearse

3 1901 05391 7466